SO RICH, SO POOR

ALSO BY PETER EDELMAN

Reconnecting Disadvantaged Young Men
(with Harry J. Holzer and Paul Offner)

Searching for America's Heart: RFK and the Renewal of Hope

Adolescence and Poverty (co-edited with Joyce Ladner)

SO RICH, SO POOR

WHY IT'S SO HARD TO END
POVERTY IN AMERICA

Peter Edelman

20 YEARS
THE NEW PRESS

Requests for permission to reproduce selections
from this book should be mailed to:
Permissions Department, The New Press, 38 Greene Street,
New York, NY 10013.

Published in the United States by The New Press, New York, 2012
Distributed by Perseus Distribution

LIBRARY OF CONGRESS CATALOGING-IN-PUBLICATION DATA

Edelman, Peter B.
So rich, so poor : why it's so hard to end poverty in America / Peter Edelman.
    p.   cm.
Includes bibliographical references and index.
ISBN 978-1-59558-785-5 (hc. : alk. paper)
1. Poverty—United States.   2. United States—Social conditions—21st
    century.   3. United States—Social policy—21st century.
    4. Poor—Government policy—United States.   I. Title.
HC110.P6E34 2012
339.4'60973—dc23   2011052784

Now in its twentieth year, The New Press publishes books that promote and enrich public discussion and understanding of the issues vital to our democracy and to a more equitable world. These books are made possible by the enthusiasm of our readers; the support of a committed group of donors, large and small; the collaboration of our many partners in the independent media and the not-for-profit sector; booksellers, who often hand-sell New Press books; librarians; and above all by our authors.

www.thenewpress.com

Composition by dix!
This book was set in Electra LT Std

Printed in the United States of America

2   4   6   8   10   9   7   5   3   1

For Ellika, Zoe, Levi, and Elijah

CONTENTS

INTRODUCTION

I had the privilege of working for Robert Kennedy in the U.S. Senate nearly half a century ago. He was a man who—arguably unlike anybody at that level since—was deeply committed to doing something very serious about poverty in this country and the intersection of poverty and race. I had the opportunity to travel the country with him, and to learn as he learned, by listening and talking to people and witnessing their struggles.

We met children suffering from extreme hunger in Mississippi and farmworkers struggling for a decent wage and the right to organize in the San Joaquin Valley of California. We worked with people pursuing community economic empowerment in the Bedford-Stuyvesant neighborhood of New York City, and we saw the enduring poverty of former coal miners striving against feudal local politics in eastern Kentucky. We encountered Native American children who had been shipped to white-run boarding schools thousands of miles from their homes and migrant farmworkers living in abandoned buses in upstate New York. I learned much more about what it's like to be poor than I could have ever learned from books.

There must have been something in me all along. I grew up Jewish in the immediate aftermath of the Holocaust and in a Minneapolis that was very anti-Semitic. I was proud that my father was appointed by then-mayor Hubert Humphrey to the Human Relations Council that he created to address the prejudice against Jews and others. And I am sure that the Holocaust shaped my sense of the vulnerability of despised minorities.

After Kennedy died, I kept finding myself reconnecting to the issues I had learned about from him and with him, especially issues about young people who don't have a fair chance. Becoming a vice president of the University of Massachusetts in the early 1970s turned out to be an avenue from which to broaden opportunities for young people. Running the juvenile corrections agency under the newly elected governor of New York Hugh Carey continued the pattern. Joining the faculty at Georgetown Law Center allowed me to teach about poverty and offer my thoughts on the written page. Going to work with Donna Shalala in the Clinton administration was a chance to work on poverty-related issues. And when I resigned from the government in protest over President Clinton's signing of the welfare law in 1996, the commitment became even more of a mission.

All along, one thing has led to another. What it adds up to is that for more than forty years I have been trying, in one way or another, to make some small difference toward reducing American poverty. Had I been part of the exodus from ancient Egypt, I would have made it to the promised land by now.

As things are, I am still at it. The purpose of this book is to look anew at why it is so hard to end American poverty and how we might do better. I write just now because poverty has steadily grown worse over the past decade, and it is more important than ever to place it on the front burner of our national concern.

I don't write with any feeling of futility. Of course, anyone who cares would wish that we had made more of a dent, but, as I'll explain, we have accomplished a lot. The idea that "nothing works" is a canard. The policy gains outweigh the policy losses by a considerable measure even with the recent deterioration of the situation. The problem is that the policy gains have been nullified by economic trends that eroded the earnings of millions while simultaneously enriching a super-elite whose wealth and income have reached unprecedented levels.

This cannot stand: "America" and "poverty" are words that

should not appear in the same sentence. We are the wealthiest country in the world; that we should have poverty at all is oxymoronic, and that we have the highest child poverty rate in the industrialized world is downright shameful.

It is not because we are not a generous nation. Americans volunteer time and donate dollars enthusiastically. They help at homeless shelters and soup kitchens; they mentor and tutor low-income children; they fund scholarships; and on and on. We have a nonprofit sector that is unequaled in the world.

But at the moment public policy is another matter entirely. Liberal members of Congress say that, just now, approaching more conservative colleagues (and not just Republicans) with a proposition that contains the word "poverty" is an immediate red flag. Homeless veterans? Maybe. Poverty? No way. And "welfare"—in the lexicon of many today, it's a pejorative.

I thought the Great Recession might renew our commitment. I thought that poverty striking millions who had assumed they were economically secure might enlist their involvement in bringing about a politics of responsiveness and empathy that would include the already poor as well as the newly impoverished. It certainly seemed so at the beginning of the Obama administration.

President Barack Obama's stimulus legislation made a surprisingly large investment not only in extended and enlarged unemployment compensation and other help for the newly unemployed, but also in measures offering significant temporary support to those who had already been struggling before the recession began. There were temporary expansions of food stamps, increases in the Earned Income Tax Credit, the Child Tax Credit, augmented housing vouchers, more help for the homeless, added funding for Head Start and child care, and more—all of which cushioned the impact of the recession on those already poor and kept as many as 7 million additional people from falling into poverty.

Still, another 9 million more people fell into poverty between 2007 and 2010. The depth of the recession called for an even more extensive effort, but what was done was impressive nonetheless.

Yet even as he took positive action, President Obama made little use of the word "poverty." The government website detailing the contents of his Recovery Act used the word "vulnerable" to characterize those portions of the legislation relating to low-income people. I was disappointed that he seldom said the "p" word, and his emphasis on the middle class with infrequent references to those at the bottom dismayed me. Our president stands in the bully pulpit, and more than anyone, he has the power to educate and lead us toward the full inclusion of every single individual in our national community.

Perhaps uttering the problematic "p" word would have jeopardized enactment of the full stimulus package, but I continue to believe that the unwillingness of our national leadership to engage the nation in a straightforward discussion of American poverty is corrosive. We proclaim our commitment to opportunity for all, but shoving one child in five under the rug in our national discourse makes a mockery of that declaration. Even now, with the resonance of "We are the 99%" and the renewed attention to inequality, scrutiny focuses more on the outsize share held by those at the top than on those floundering at the bottom. The discussion must be placed in the broader context of economic inequality and social immobility, but the grim present and possibly grimmer future of the millions in poverty must be an explicit part of it.

We have become more and more ensconced in what Paul Krugman calls a "two-speed world." We are a society of dichotomies: of gated communities and ghastly ghettoes; of yachts and people with no buoys at all; of private jets and children whose wings are clipped early, long before they could even consider flying. We need a more honest and more candid discussion, and we need it sooner rather than later.

Whether President Obama was right or wrong for not addressing poverty more straightforwardly in that political moment, things still turned sour quite quickly. The attitude of much of the public hardened even toward the victims of the recession. Phony deficit hawks proclaimed the need for immediate austerity to preclude fiscal Armageddon and found a ready audience. The already poor, on the screen ever so briefly in the wake of Obama's victory, fell from public view.

And since the summer of 2011, with the terrible budget agreement struck to get the debt ceiling increased, with the disastrous condition of state and local treasuries, and with the continuing weakness of the economy, the poor face the worst of what looks like a long siege for a large segment of our population. Job prospects are dismal. The Republicans' refusal even to consider revenue increases while demanding sharp deficit reduction portends deeper and deeper cuts at the federal level in programs for the poor. And flat-broke state and local governments, some with evident enthusiasm, have taken a meat ax to programs that would reduce the pain.

It has always been hard to galvanize broad support for public policy directed at reducing poverty. Too many Americans are skeptical about public policy to help the poor, especially as they view the "poor" in their mind's eye. Beginning with the Bible and continuing through the Elizabethan poor laws, throughout history there has been an instinctive belief among some that the poor have no one to blame but themselves. A special version of this illusion exists in the United States, the Horatio Alger mythology that one makes it (or doesn't) on his or her own. The pioneer spirit and rugged individualism—values to be admired on the whole—contribute to the American version of the "blame the poor" story.

We need to be clear that public policy has indeed made a huge difference in the lives of poor people, beginning with the New Deal. Starting with the Social Security Act of 1935, continuing with the burst of activity in the 1960s, and on from there, we actually have made great progress—in steps sometimes not noticed by the general public that are often done incrementally and in fits and starts when an opportunity presents itself, yet progress that is vital for those who benefit. That we already have multiple policies and programs that are effective in reducing poverty is a major point of this book.

We did enact Medicaid and the Children's Health Insurance

Program (CHIP), and many health indicators for low-income people did improve. We enacted food stamps, and the near-starvation conditions we saw in some parts of the country were ameliorated. We enacted the Earned Income Tax Credit and the Child Tax Credit, and the incomes of low-wage workers with children have climbed. We enacted Pell Grants, and millions of people can afford college who otherwise could not possibly attend. We enacted Supplementary Security Income (SSI), and the income floor rose for elderly and disabled people whose earnings from work didn't provide enough social security. And there is much more — housing vouchers, Head Start, child care assistance, and legal services for the poor, to name a few. Despite its aversion to discussing poverty, the Obama administration and Congress also added 16 million people to Medicaid in the Affordable Care Act, appropriated billions to improve the education of low-income children, and spent a stunning amount on the least well off — more than $150 billion — in the so-called Recovery Act.

To suggest dismissively — as so many conservatives do — that "we waged a war on poverty, and poverty won" simply because there is still poverty is like saying the Clean Air and Clean Water Acts failed because there is still pollution. Yet poverty is in the ascendancy just now.

WHAT IS IN THIS BOOK

I make four major points in this book about what has happened and what we still need to do. From the vantage point of 1968, where we were when Robert Kennedy died, there have been a lot of surprises as we moved down the road. I suppose any present tends to frame our ideas of the future; that was certainly the case with me. I did not foresee much of what transpired after 1968 that would curtail our ability to continue the progress of the mid-1960s.

So my first major point is that we have to understand why, despite the achievements of the New Deal, the Great Society, and since, we still have so much poverty. Three forces — all unforeseen in large measure in 1968—account for the course of American poverty over the past forty years. Most important of those is the fundamental change that occurred in the American economy. Good-paying low-skill jobs went overseas and gave way to automation, and low-wage work became ubiquitous. Millions of people are worse off now than their parents were, and even more millions are on a treadmill to nowhere. Second is the substantial increase in the number of families headed by a single parent, usually a woman. The plethora of low-wage jobs has made it more and more difficult for a family with only one wage-earner to make ends meet. Third is the fact that race and gender still matter a great deal as to who is poor and who is not. Despite important improvement in the 1990s, minorities and single women with children continue to be vastly poorer than are whites and married couples, and attitudes about race and gender are still major drivers of the politics of poverty.

Second, the topic is not just poverty. Even more serious is the ever-increasing number of people in extreme poverty: people living below half the poverty line, or less than $9,000 for a family of three. An astonishing 20.5 million people lived in extreme poverty in 2010, up by nearly 8 million in just ten years, and 6 million had no income other than food stamps. At the same time, people who are not poor but nonetheless routinely struggle to stay afloat also need much more of our attention. Adding in the near-poor—those with incomes below twice the poverty line or $44,000 for a family of four—brings the total of the poor and the near-poor to more than 103 million people, a number that is nearly as arresting as the utterly shocking number who are in extreme poverty.

Third, the stunning ascendancy of the wealthiest people must be addressed; it has become a moral issue as well as one of politics and economics. The American economy did not stagnate over the past forty years: it grew, but the fruits of that growth went to those at the top. I used to believe that the debate over wealth distribution should be conducted separately from the poverty debate, in order to minimize the attacks on antipoverty advocates for engaging in "class warfare." But now we literally cannot afford to separate the two issues. The economic and political power of those at the top is not only eroding our democracy but also making it virtually impossible to find the resources to do more at the bottom. Nor is the issue merely about those at the bottom: today's inequality hurts a substantial majority of Americans.

The dangers that the top poses to the rest of us appeared in new form during the disastrous housing bubble. Having used their political power to dismantle key elements of regulation originally enacted as far back as the New Deal, the people at the top—aided by a small army of eager and equally greedy foot soldiers—caused predatory, subprime, and just unconscionably reckless loans to be made to millions of people who ended up losing everything. Perhaps some among the creators of the new mortgage-backed securities rationalized that they had discovered a way to create wealth for those whose incomes had been stuck or declining for decades, but many knew full well that they were taking from the less affluent for their own advantage.

Fourth, if we want to make greater progress on poverty, bold action will be required on many fronts: public policy and private action, national and local initiatives, and steps across many fields of endeavor—income from work, work supports like child care, safety-net measures, health, housing, criminal justice reform, human services of all kinds, and investments in education and child development. Public policy is essential, but so is civic action. The millions of one-on-one, one-by-one connections that occur every day, both professionally and through volunteering, make a huge difference. Individual responsibility is indispensable, too, a fact that should not even have to be spoken out loud. And, right now, we still need significant steps to put America back to work. It is unacceptable that so many members of Congress reject those ideas out of hand; we must make sure they are held to public account.

We have two immediate priorities in addition to the pressing tasks of getting our people back to work and protecting what we already do to keep people out of poverty. Both priorities involve attacking the blatant inequality of today: one, to see that the wealth-iest Americans and big corporations pay at least as much in taxes as they did before 2001; and two, to address the worst of our poverty—the 6 million people who have no income other than food stamps and the 20.5 million who live in deep poverty.

These matters are particularly urgent today. From the 1960s to 2000, we held our own in the struggle against poverty, albeit with serious setbacks in the 1980s. The twenty-first century is something else again, so far. All of the indicators of poverty and economic diffi-culty show us headed in the wrong direction since the millennium and have accelerated significantly in recent years. The recession has been declared officially "over," yet poverty has continued to increase. Prospects for change for the better in the near future are bleak.

We also need to face the fact that this time—this century—may not be like times past. The jobs we have lost may never come back in full measure. The future may be one not only of more low-wage jobs but also of not enough jobs, period. It is increasingly a fic-tion that everyone has a chance to move up. We are likely to need a much more muscular effort to share our nation's largesse more fully. The question of whether we can find the will to act is ever more pressing.

1

A Snapshot of Our Current Mess

Two stories sum up the contrast between the appalling current facts about poverty itself and the equally appalling current facts about the politics of poverty.

The first story is about poverty itself—in particular, the poorest of the poor.

Jason DeParle is a remarkable journalist. He cares deeply about poverty, which in and of itself is distinctive, and he is smart, creative, and thorough. And he writes for the *New York Times*, which gives him a twofold advantage: the resources necessary to do big projects and an audience as wide as a print journalist can get.

At some point in 2009, DeParle began to wonder how well the nation's safety net was functioning to ameliorate the impact of the recession, especially food stamps (now called the Supplemental Nutrition Assistance Program, or SNAP). He knew that the food stamp rolls had skyrocketed during the recession, but he wanted to know more about state and local variations in their availability and the reasons why, going beyond the data the federal government collects from the states. So he contacted each state to ask for its data. He was frequently told the information was confidential; sometimes he had to threaten a freedom-of-information suit. On other occasions, he had to go up the chain of command, go to the legislature, or threaten to do so, but one way or another he did obtain the data. The result was a powerful series illustrated by stories of individuals coping as best they could. He learned even more than he expected.

DeParle was looking for details on the reasons for state-by-state and local variations, but the most important thing he unearthed was truly astonishing. The data included the incomes of applicants, and as of 2009 there were 2 million families, comprising 6 million people, whose only income was from food stamps.[1] If anything, the numbers are even higher as I write this two years later.

How could this be? The answer is in what has happened to welfare, or Temporary Assistance to Needy Families (TANF), as it is now called. The key point is that while there is a legal right to receive food stamps, there is no longer a legal right to obtain welfare. When President Bill Clinton signed TANF into law in 1996, he didn't just end welfare as we knew it. The process that he set in motion brought a virtual end to cash help for low-income families with children in much of the country. When the Great Recession came along, the government safety net for families with children had a huge hole.

So SNAP is the one income assistance program we have that is (almost) universally available based on need. You walk into the office (or, even better, use one of the rapidly expanding avenues to apply for the benefits electronically), and they have to give you the benefits that the law says you are guaranteed. Also, because the federal government pays the full cost of the benefits (but not all of the administrative costs), it's free money for the states (although, even so, state participation rates vary widely, with, for example, as few as half of eligible Californians receiving it).

Of course, food stamps provide an income that is nowhere near enough to live on, because their purpose is only to help alleviate hunger. The benefit for a family of three with no other income is $526 a month, or $6328 annually.[2] That figure is about one-third of a poverty-level income, and even that is a level temporarily enhanced by the Recovery Act. But it is a legally mandated entitlement.

When George W. Bush took office, there were 17.2 million people receiving food stamps, a figure that had decreased every year

since 1995. This re ˙   ny improved
through the last half   d all the way
down to the people ɪ   ts in the program that were part   eligibility. By
2007, the number h   lue in part to
the steadily deterioɪ   le beginning
in 2001 and, very im   cision by the
Bush administration   od-stamp eligibility and benefit levels. President Bush was no friend of the poor
in many respects, but he was a much more progressive president on
food stamps than President Clinton.

As of May 2011, the program had expanded for thirty-seven con-
secutive months, with twenty thousand recipients added every day.
By the fall of 2011, the figure was close to 46 million; one in seven
people, and one in four children, were receiving food stamps.[3]

So SNAP has been a powerful antirecessionary force. The SNAP
half of the story is the good half.

Now for the other half—the reason why there could be 6 million people with no income other than food stamps. The big story
is what's happened to cash assistance. Food stamps went from
26.3 million to 46 million recipients as the recession took hold and
persisted. But the needle measuring welfare barely moved. In October 2007, there were 3.9 million mothers and children receiving
TANF, down from more than 14 million in the early 1990s. Three
years later, with unemployment still in the stratosphere, the number on TANF had only risen slightly, to 4.5 million, even though
there were plenty of people who needed help and states had funding to help if they wanted to.[4] When barely 1 percent of the population is getting cash assistance, food stamps are the only source of
help for far too many people. Whatever the efficacy of the safety net
for the "better off" poor—with the Earned Income Tax Credit and
the Child Tax Credit (as well as food stamps) as income supplements for people who have income from work—people at the very
bottom who have little (if any) work are mainly eligible only for
food stamps.

Why is welfare not of any use in a recession and barely relevant in many states even when there is no recession? Two reasons: one, as mentioned, there is no longer a legal entitlement to welfare; and two, the culture in welfare offices across most of the country is one of turning people away. In some places, there is an apparent paradox: a pride in a state or county's outreach efforts to help people obtain food stamps and a simultaneous policy of turning away people who apply for TANF. (On a closer look, the difference is not so paradoxical. States get a bonus for doing outreach on food stamps. By contrast, they receive what amounts to a bonus for keeping people off the TANF rolls. This is because the funding they get from the federal government remains constant regardless of the size of the caseload. The fewer people on the rolls, the more money they have to use for other purposes.)

Food stamps: 26.3 million to 46 million. TANF: 3.9 million to 4.5 million. Striking, to say the least.

The bottom line is that Jason DeParle found that there are 6 million people in our country whose only income is food stamps. Two percent of our people. One in every fifty.

Let us now shift the scene to a hearing room in the House of Representatives on June 1, 2011, to an event styled "A Hearing on Federal Welfare Programs." The body holding the hearing is the Subcommittee on Regulatory Affairs, Stimulus Oversight, and Government Spending. Chairing the hearing is Representative Jim Jordan, Republican from Ohio, who describes himself on his website as "one of the most conservative members of Congress." The specific focus is a new study from the Government Accountability Office that analyzed duplicative programs in the federal government.[5]

Jordan is the chair of an important subcommittee in the Congress. He has power. His witness, Robert Rector of the Heritage Foundation, is a leading conservative advocate on poverty issues. He has significant public visibility.

Framing the issue, Jordan says, "Since Lyndon Johnson declared a war on poverty in 1964, Americans have spent $16 trillion on welfare at the state and local level." Actually, no. Not even close. It is true that we have spent a lot of money to alleviate and reduce poverty, and we would have had massively more poverty without those programs. But Jordan does not differentiate among the programs and their accomplishments or failures. To him, they are all just "welfare." (Nor does he acknowledge that welfare itself has actually shrunk by two-thirds since the mid-1990s.)

Jordan's agenda becomes more transparent when he introduces Rector. Jordan opines that, "for all programs across all those agencies, we send the wrong incentives. I've often said that the welfare system particularly says to the single mom out there, don't get married, don't get a job, have more kids and you get more money. And is that a fair assessment of . . . these hundred plus programs sending the wrong message . . . [?]"

Rector's reply: "All of these programs have an anti-marriage effect." Rector does go on at length, but that first sentence of his reply says it all. Bear in mind that the programs Rector says have an "anti-marriage effect" span everything from a preschooler's Head Start and job retraining for a displaced factory worker to Medicaid for a widow in a nursing home or hospice.

Six million people whose only income is food stamps and 20.5 million in deep poverty. To see the conversation at the hearing as detached from reality is an understatement and then some.

2

What We Have Accomplished

FOOD STAMPS—A SUCCESS STORY

In April 1967, Robert Kennedy went to Mississippi as part of a series of hearings around the country to build support for the reauthorization of the Economic Opportunity Act of 1964—the war on poverty. Mississippi had the largest Head Start program anywhere. It was widely heralded in the civil rights and antipoverty world, but it was in deep political trouble. The law gave the federal government the power to bypass any governor who refused the federal money and award it directly to nonprofit organizations. That had happened in Mississippi, and the Child Development Group of Mississippi (CDGM) was the result—a twenty-one-county program that for a time was the largest employer in the state. Nor was CDGM just big; its leadership and many of its employees were veterans of the civil rights movement. Governor Paul B. Johnson Jr.— who had succeeded the better-known Ross Barnett—was furious and enlisted the state's powerful senators to pressure President Lyndon B. Johnson to cut off CDGM's funding. Kennedy went to Mississippi to show support for CDGM.

But the trip turned out to be about something else entirely: children, thousands of them, hungry to a point very near starvation. Why? To put it simply, the white power structure in Mississippi— conscious of what the recently enacted Voting Rights Act of 1965 might do to their hold on the heavily African American state—was trying to drive out as many African Americans as possible. A number of factors had come together. The previous year, Congress had extended the minimum wage to farmworkers. Nationwide, only the largest 1 percent of all the nation's farms and only one-third of all farmworkers were affected, but a disproportionate number of those farms were in Mississippi. At about the same time, machines to pick the cotton had become available, and chemicals to kill the boll weevils instead of going after them by hand had also come into greater use. Consequently, the marginally more expensive farm labor could be dispensed with and those who lived on plantations could be evicted.

Their incomes gone, the families had nowhere to turn. Welfare — though it was a pittance then, as it is now — was totally unavailable to two-parent families, which the affected families overwhelmingly were. Surplus commodities, formerly available pretty easily, were being replaced by the recently enacted food stamps program, then a small-scale initiative that was reaching barely 2 million people nationally but had been put in place widely in most of Mississippi. The surplus commodities were less than palatable — the wheat and bulgur were often maggot-infested and hardly enough to live on — but you could get them by going to a warehouse near the train station and they were free.

In contrast to such access, to obtain food stamps one had to go to an office and apply to welfare functionaries who were hostile to the new program in general and to African American applicants in particular. Even more important, one had to pay for the food stamps, a charge that had a big effect on participation in every place where the change in programs occurred. The fee schedule began at zero income with a charge of $2 per person in the family. People with a zero income — thought by the bureaucrats at the Department of Agriculture in Washington to be a purely hypothetical category — actually did exist in Mississippi.

The result — with no jobs, no welfare, no surplus commodities, and no food stamps — was widespread hunger and severe malnutrition. Kennedy and the other senators were accompanied by Daniel

Schorr and his CBS cameras on a trip to the Mississippi Delta to see for themselves children with swollen bellies and running sores on their arms and legs that did not heal—and the entire nation saw that evening what Kennedy had seen earlier that day. (Civil rights lawyer Marian Wright, my future wife whom I had met just three days earlier, served as his guide.)

Kennedy was deeply moved and outraged. His children remember him telling them at dinner the next night that they had to make themselves a part of doing something about this—a rare outburst in a house where the expectation of public service usually went without saying. The very next day, he went to see Secretary of Agriculture Orville Freeman. I was there when he bluntly told the former Minnesota governor and early backer of his brother John F. Kennedy for president, "Orville, you've got to get some food down there." Freeman responded by changing the requirement that families with no income had to pay for their food stamps, a step that was within his power to take without amending the law. It was a small first step, but symbolically a very large and important one.

Kennedy put relieving hunger at the top of his list. His suggestion led to the Field Foundation (which was founded by the liberal New York branch of the Chicago retailing family and went out of business in 1988) sending a group of physicians to Mississippi to examine hundreds of children and to document the degree of their malnutrition. When their report came back with shocking data on the incidence of exotic diseases like marasmus and kwashiorkor as well as rickets and other indicia of severe malnutrition, he arranged a Senate hearing to which he invited Mississippi's senators, who actually showed up. Senator John Stennis was embarrassed, enough so that he proposed an emergency appropriation of $10 million.

Kennedy also got a friend at CBS to commission a documentary. Completed following his death, it showed a child dying on camera in a San Antonio hospital after being born severely malnourished. Jamie Whitten, the powerful Mississippi congressman who chaired the House Appropriations Subcommittee on Agriculture, unleashed an investigation of the film to find out whether its stories had been staged. The documentary, shockingly stark, was definitely effective.

Kennedy told me to look into the scope of the problem around the country, and we found out quickly that serious hunger was not confined to Mississippi. He assigned me to work on setting up more trips to help him focus the country's attention on the extent of the problem. We looked at both South Carolina and eastern Kentucky. His friend Senator Ernest "Fritz" Hollings of South Carolina begged him not to publicize the shortcomings of that state and promised to take leadership on the issue (which he did do after Kennedy died). Kennedy did not go to South Carolina, but he did go to eastern Kentucky, where he was followed by a massive press posse, given that the trip occurred in February 1968, when speculation about whether he would run for president was at a fever pitch. Having advanced the trip carefully before deciding finally to go, we found exactly what we knew we would find: there also was a most serious hunger problem in eastern Kentucky.

We traveled across a stretch of communities, holding hearings in one-room schoolhouses, a high school gymnasium, and a college auditorium, and visited families in their homes, hearing of people's struggles firsthand. The basic problem was that the closing of the coal mines had left thousands with no income from work. Welfare was limited to single-parent families and was a pittance in any case, and food assistance was spotty at best. Many families had left for points north in search of a better life, but that could not be a solution for everyone. Representative Carl Perkins had steered various job-training programs to the region, and the favored few survived by participating in successive trainings. For the most part, though, the feudal sway of the local political barons and their cronies left ordinary people on the outside looking in. As in Mississippi, politics had a great deal to do with the widespread incidence of egregious hunger in Kentucky.

That was the last trip Kennedy was able to make; he jumped into the presidential race in March and was killed in June. But he had launched a process that proved to be enormously successful.

Senator George McGovern picked up the mantle, becoming chair of a newly minted Special Committee on Hunger and Malnutrition. The Field Foundation's financing of advocacy continued as well, with a Citizens Commission on Hunger report that attracted wide attention. President Richard Nixon—prodded by his first secretary of agriculture, Clifford Hardin, a former president of the University of Nebraska and a longtime advocate against global hunger—sent to Congress the first-ever presidential message on hunger. (President Johnson, spiteful because it was Robert Kennedy who had brought the problem to national attention, had refused to do anything on the issue.)

Fritz Hollings kept his promise. It was most likely not an entirely selfless act, but it was important regardless of his motives. Southern Democrats were in something of a bind. In the wake of the Voting Rights Act, they needed an issue (if they could see beyond the end of their noses) with which to appeal to the African American vote without losing the white vote. They couldn't embrace civil rights legislation directly, but feeding hungry people would be all right. Hollings took a hunger tour of South Carolina and pronounced himself appalled (as he no doubt was) by what he had seen.

Hollings needed to convince his fellow southerners that it was in their interest to act. The southern members of Congress controlled the Agriculture Committees on both sides of the Hill, bodies through which any legislation to alleviate hunger would have to pass. Had they decided to play the race card and stand in the way, it would have been difficult to get a bill enacted; pressed by Hollings, however, the committees acted—led in particular by Senator Herman Talmadge of Georgia, the chair of the Senate committee and a die-hard segregationist (in contrast to the more moderate Hollings). Civil rights would ultimately hand the South to the Republicans, but responding to hunger may have slowed arrival of the day of reckoning because it helped attract African American voters to go to the polls and vote for the Democrats.

None of the movement forward was automatic. Senator McGovern's special committee held hearings around the country and issued numerous reports that received extensive publicity. By 1971, legislation creating national standards for the program and limiting the purchase price for the stamps to 30 percent of a family's income was enacted. Further legislation in 1973 (after Senator McGovern had been the 1972 Democratic candidate for president) required that the program become national by July 1, 1974. This was extremely important because rural counties in many states across the country had up to then refused to have food stamps in their domains. The final building block, a 1977 law passed at the initiative of President Jimmy Carter, eliminated the purchase requirement, so that stamps would be issued based simply on a family's income.

Support for food stamps has until now been bipartisan throughout the history of the program, with Senator Bob Dole of Kansas the most notable Republican advocate. When President Ronald Reagan and Senator Jesse Helms proposed deep cuts to food stamps in 1981, Dole's leadership in the newly Republican majority Senate was the key to stemming the tide, although dramatic cuts were made nonetheless. Significant cuts—$27 billion over the first six years—were again made in the 1996 welfare law, and only about half have been fully restored. By contrast, President George W. Bush supported the program to a surprising extent, one of the reasons the rolls increased while he was in office even before the recession. But now we see House Republicans trying to turn the program into a block grant—in effect cutting benefits by capping them—just when SNAP (just to reiterate, the current name for food stamps) has been a lifeline to millions.

SNAP is unquestionably a successful public policy story. Its original expansion and maturation to nationwide status under a Republican president is a case study in effective advocacy. It provides a small underpinning of income to those who have no other income, and it is an important income supplement for struggling low-wage workers. It brings almost all poor people together within a single benefit structure and has also now proven itself to be a powerful tool to cushion the devastating force of our Great Recession.

Why is SNAP such a success, especially in comparison to

welfare? For one thing, fighting hunger is more attractive politically than handing out cash. It has more instinctive appeal and tends to assure voters that the aid is less likely to be abused. Beyond that, nearly every antipoverty success over the past half century has marched under a banner other than fighting poverty: health care, housing, education, the elderly, child care—and hunger. I am quite aware of my earlier statement declaring my displeasure with the absence of leaders like Robert Kennedy and Paul Wellstone who stand up and say unequivocally that poverty is unacceptable. But in our current political world, it works better to call it by other names.

The political decision of the Bush administration to support food stamps is a perfect example of this. The Newt Gingrich–Rudy Giuliani camp had denounced food stamps as "welfare" and set out to destroy the program (an attitude that has resurfaced in the current Tea Party–driven House of Representatives). The Bush-Bloomberg camp embraced it as "nutritional assistance" and worked to expand it, with Bush giving bonuses to states that enrolled more people. This support was in part the doing of Eric Bost, a Texan close to President Bush and the undersecretary in charge of the program at the Department of Agriculture, but it also shows that nomenclature matters.

Of course, the whole food stamp story is also deeply rooted in the self-interest of groups with political clout. The food industry supports food stamps. Farmers, processors and manufacturers, and grocers have all supported food stamps (although farmers—wanting to preserve their own subsidies—have been less supportive in recent years). This kind of backing is not invariably a guarantee of success, but it does always help, and in the case of SNAP—along with the moral sense that no one should go hungry—it has definitely worked.

THE WAR ON POVERTY AND
THE GREAT SOCIETY

We could start a history of poverty policy with the Bible, and of course some of the key building blocks of our federal safety net, patchwork though it is, were enacted as part of the New Deal. But if our mission is to understand why it has been so hard to reduce poverty further since it reached its historic low of 11.1 percent in 1973, our discussion should begin with the 1960s. In a very real sense, the 1960s were the beginning of the modern American history of anti-poverty policy and, concomitantly, of the modern American history of the politics of poverty. Most of us remember Reagan's declaration that "we fought a war on poverty and poverty won." Fewer are aware that the poverty rate actually dropped spectacularly in the 1960s, going from 22.4 percent in 1959—the first year for which we have poverty statistics—to the 11.1 percent of 1973.

There were millions in poverty in the 1930s because the economy had collapsed. There were still millions in poverty in the 1960s, albeit fewer millions, but it was now poverty in the midst of plenty, a novel American phenomenon. Initiatives to deal with that poverty were a new venture.

With the advent of the 1960s, we turned a page—one that had begun to turn with the *Brown v. Board* decision in 1954 and the first highly publicized student civil rights sit-ins in Greensboro, North Carolina, in early 1960. Spurred by the civil rights movement, Americans began to develop an awareness of the inequality in their midst, not only racial inequality but also inequality of income. John F. Kennedy's campaign in West Virginia is said to have opened his eyes to white poverty, and Michael Harrington's now-classic *The Other America* captured a surprising degree of attention.

Newly in office as the attorney general, Robert Kennedy installed his high school friend David Hackett in an office opening directly into his and charged Hackett with developing a program to reduce juvenile delinquency. The cadre of experts Hackett assembled from inside and outside the government developed key aspects of what became the war on poverty, with White House involvement increasing in 1963 and the White House taking over the planning after President Kennedy's assassination. At the last

Cabinet meeting before he was murdered, Kennedy is said to have been doodling the word "poverty."

President Johnson dragooned Kennedy's brother-in-law R. Sargent Shriver to take over the responsibility, assigning to him the tasks of getting legislation drafted and of setting up the new agency, all without leaving his already demanding position as director of the Peace Corps. After a frenetic six weeks of effort, the bill was sent to Congress in March 1964. On August 20, President Johnson signed into law the Economic Opportunity Act, and implementation of it followed at a similarly dizzying pace. The war on poverty was of course not a single program but an array of individual programs, each of which required major effort to make it operational.

To those involved, the new law was truly a war on poverty, and confidence abounded that it was a war that would be won (putting aside our unfortunate American penchant for calling major initiatives "wars"). Objectively, it was not a war but rather a collection of skirmishes, although it is also true that the energy it unleashed created an important sense of empowerment in low-income communities and helped produce a new generation of leaders who went on to hold public offices and to stay involved civically throughout their lives—important outcomes that should not be minimized.

At its heart, the war on poverty was a strategy of opportunity and support services of various kinds—a basket of programs to mold children, youth, and young adults into capable people who could function successfully in the job market and be good citizens. It was coupled with legal services to challenge practices both private and public that victimized the poor and also with health clinics to improve access to medical care. And it was topped off by a dash—a highly controversial dash, as it turned out—of community organizing to help the poor gain political efficacy to improve their lives, both personally and communally. It was not focused directly on creating jobs and raising incomes. The theory of the case was that the tax cut of 1964 would warm up the economy and create the necessary jobs.

Signing the Economic Opportunity Act, President Johnson said,

"[T]he measure . . . offers the answer that its title implies—the answer of opportunity. For the purpose of the Economic [Opportunity] Act of 1964 is to offer opportunity, not an opiate."[1] Nor was President Johnson obfuscating the facts. The strategy of the war on poverty was primarily one of opening the door of opportunity to all Americans.

Head Start was the positive poster child of the poverty war, the one piece that Reagan deemed acceptable. Not surprisingly, Americans have instinctive sympathy for a program that gives young children a "head start" in being prepared for school. There were politicized critiques of particular local programs, as in Mississippi, but they disappeared as time passed (although significant questions about the quality of some local programs are still extant). The good news about Head Start now is that it reaches about half the eligible children in the country; of course, the fact that it reaches only half is also the bad news.

The negative poster child of the poverty war was community action, an alternative human-service delivery system based in low-income neighborhoods to serve their residents. A key idea behind it—that the people who would benefit from it would have a major say in its operation—was idealistic. Its core organizational point was that traditional social service agencies had too often drawn a red line around low-income neighborhoods, especially neighborhoods of color, and would not serve those who lived there. The new local agency would receive funds directly from the federal government, bypassing city hall. Its governance was to involve the "maximum feasible participation" of the poor to avoid capture by local political bosses who might see a new opportunity for patronage or revenue.

Many mayors and other elected officials were infuriated. New federal money was coming to town, and they had no say in how it was spent. In some places, community action agency staffers took residents downtown to voice their grievances at city hall, often not at all decorously. Nor did the backlash come only from public officials. Landlords bridled at rent strikes organized by community action employees, and growers saw the hand of antipoverty activists in fomenting dissent among migrant farmworkers.

Congress responded by amending the law to permit mayoral or county government control of the community action agencies, and the confrontational behavior quickly ended. Nonetheless, it was the early missteps of some local community action agencies that gave the entire program a bad name.

Trouble also came for the federal funding of lawyers who represented poor people and their organizations in civil cases against state and local governments, agribusiness and landlords, and even the federal government itself. That the program—reframed in 1974 as the Legal Services Corporation—still exists, albeit with less funding and subject to restrictions on the categories of cases its lawyers can handle, is largely attributable to the staunch support over the years of the American Bar Association.

The rest of the war on poverty was, in the main, less controversial. Job Corps is now funded at about $1.7 billion annually. It is expensive because it is a residential program, but it is widely regarded as worthwhile. VISTA (Volunteers in Service to America) experienced controversy in the 1960s because of the activist behavior of some of its volunteers, but it nevertheless became a component of the AmeriCorps program enacted at the behest of President Clinton. Upward Bound and Foster Grandparents still operate and are very popular. The Community Health Centers program, now based in the Department of Health and Human Services with an annual budget in excess of $2 billion, enjoys broad bipartisan support.

So the "war on poverty" was not an all-out war on poverty, nor would it have been even if it had been funded at levels far beyond those of the 1960s. Many of its programs were excellent and did make a great difference in the lives of millions of people, but it was not a strategy that could ever have come close to eradicating American poverty.

What about President Johnson's Great Society, which dwarfed the war on poverty in size and scope? When we talk of the Great

Society, we are talking about Medicare, Medicaid, the historic civil rights laws of the period, federal aid to education, housing and community development programs, employment and training programs beyond Job Corps, and more. The list includes far-reaching accomplishments that have been critically important for low-income people.

The 1960s were truly a historic decade of progress on civil rights and poverty. President Johnson deserves great credit for what was done under his leadership; second only to Abraham Lincoln, he was our greatest president on civil rights. His achievements with regard to poverty are very important, too, although sullied in the eyes of many by the weakness of his response to the underlying causes of the unprecedented civil unrest that swept the inner cities of the country throughout his presidency.

When all of its programs are added in, can we say that the Great Society amounted to a war on poverty? After all, poverty was cut in half between 1959 and 1973. Why did poverty drop so impressively in the 1960s?

Although the Great Society is certainly part of it, the answer is complicated. So is the broader historical framework. The economy had boomed since World War II. There had been some inflation and a couple of recessions, but the postwar period was truly a time when a rising tide lifted all boats. The real incomes of people at the bottom, including minorities, grew. Union membership exceeded 30 percent of the workforce. There had been trepidation that the demobilization of the war effort would create economic slack, but meeting pent-up housing and consumer needs at home and postwar reconstruction abroad kept things humming. The war-torn economies of other nations left the United States facing little competition on the global playing field. The GI Bill pumped money into higher education and also created opportunities. Women who had worked in the war plants obligingly returned to homemaking, and men were in general able to support their families with the income they brought in. But not everyone benefited. The poor were out there; they just needed to be seen.

The economy was in a slack period when President Kennedy was elected, but the generally upward trajectory of the postwar years was still operative. Civil rights and antipoverty advocacy began to intersect, as civil rights activists realized that having the right to sit at a lunch counter didn't mean a person had the money to pay for a meal. The March on Washington in 1963 was a March for Jobs and Freedom. The main grievance of the civil unrest that swept the nation's inner cities was about jobs. The Poor People's Campaign that Dr. King was leading when he was murdered was a campaign for economic justice. The civil rights and antipoverty legislation of the 1960s, together with movement advocacy and changing public attitudes, opened labor markets to African Americans and others who had been left behind by the rising tide.

The powerful civil rights laws, especially the ban on employment discrimination in the Civil Rights Act of 1964, were instrumental in opening employers' doors. Big-city mayors—pressured by activists and organizers (some of them employees of community action agencies)—hired large numbers of people of color. African American poverty fell from 55.1 percent in 1959 to 33.5 percent in 1970. The improved employment results contributed to that change, along with the increased wages of workers who had migrated from the rural south to the urban north and west.

The opening of the welfare rolls was another major factor. The number of people on welfare went from 3 million in 1960 to 8.5 million in 1970, an increase that substantially augmented family incomes in many states and contributed to the reduction of poverty. Welfare did not raise a family's income above poverty by itself, but it could bring a partial check to supplement a low-wage job and could add to the resources of an extended family. It contributed particularly to the reduction of African American poverty, because African Americans had been disproportionately denied assistance over the years. Coupled with a robust jobs policy, welfare is a necessary element of an antipoverty strategy, and what happened in the 1960s is an apt illustration of this point.

The civil rights movement and community action activists

stimulated, directly and indirectly, the formation of a welfare rights movement, which in turn reached low-income mothers and inspired them to march on welfare offices and demand assistance. In some cities, welfare bureaucracies were newly responsive because their mayors were feeling political pressure. The new cadre of legal services lawyers advised people that qualifying applicants had a legal right to receive benefits and went to court when welfare officials did not respond. The advice was validated when the issue reached the Supreme Court under Chief Justice Earl Warren in 1968. In the first case about welfare to reach the court in the thirty-three years of the law's existence, the court ruled that the Social Security Act did indeed provide a legal entitlement to help.

The near-tripling of the welfare rolls in one decade occurred mainly because there was a large backlog of women—disproportionately African American—who had always been eligible for benefits but who had been turned down in a world in which welfare officials were regarded as having total discretion to help or not as they deemed. Unfortunately, though, the welfare agencies' liberalized according of cash assistance did not include much help for women to get jobs and get off the rolls once on. As a result, the newly enlarged rolls stayed large, and the political backlash against welfare that brought the Reagan cuts of 1981 and eventuated in the welfare law of 1996 began.

If the programs of the 1960s do not add up to a war on poverty or account by themselves for the big drop in poverty during that decade, does adding in everything else that has been enacted between 1935 and the present add up to a coherent set of policies to fight poverty, a serious "war on poverty," if you will?

The answer is "yes," but it is a heavily qualified yes. The American framework is a patchwork, not a coherent weave of policies, but it contains important pieces that do make a big difference. The programs do not follow a blueprint. They were enacted in fits and spurts beginning in 1935 and continuing to the present day. Some of what we have is excellent public policy, yet there are also enormous gaps. Unlike the Europeans, who are much more systematic in their approaches, we have done well in some areas but horribly in others.

The elderly are viewed as the most deserving and so are cared for the best in our public policy, although Social Security and Medicare are under attack now. The disabled have achieved a status as modestly deserving, we might say. People who have children and work at poorly paying jobs get some help. Children are nonetheless the poorest age group because too many of their parents cannot find full-time work or have no job at all and are seen in our politics as undeserving, especially if they are single mothers. Working-age nondisabled adults who have no children (or no custodial children) have always been seen as the least deserving, although single mothers with children are hardly the "apple of America's political eye," so to speak.

If there is an impression that the New Deal and the 1960s were the Golden Age after which we stopped creating public policy helpful to low-income people, it is quite wrong. The Nixon period was one of extensive legislation to help low-income people (in a time when Congress was controlled by the Democrats), including a proposal he made for a guaranteed minimum income for families with children that was not enacted. President Reagan is not an exemplar of concern for low-income people, but, even so, he signed a tax reform bill that relieved millions of low-income people from paying federal income taxes (a provision that is now, ironically, the subject of a Republican backlash) and also signed major Medicaid expansions every year from 1984 through 1988. The first Bush administration saw significant child care legislation, and President Clinton achieved a major expansion of the Earned Income Tax Credit and enactment of the Children's Health Insurance Program (as well as the more controversial 1996 welfare law). And of course President Obama secured passage of a truly historic health care law that adds 16 million low-income adults to Medicaid.

So we have accomplished a great deal. But there are two huge fissures in our national income support structure and a number of other gaps we must fill. One is the enormous hole in our response to the 20.5 million people who have incomes below half the poverty line (although our help to people between 50 and 100 percent of the poverty line is hardly adequate). The second is the inadequacy of the support we offer to ensure that low-wage workers receive a living income. There is much more, of course, going beyond weak policies about income—a criminal justice system that incarcerates too many in general and especially locks up people of color, a continuing shortfall in our attention to the inner city and suburban and rural areas of concentrated poverty, and the still-elusive goal of giving every child a quality education.

Nevertheless, before we turn to a discussion of where we went wrong, it is vital to understand what we have done well. The framework we have, flawed as it is, kept some 40 million people out of poverty in 2010[2]—close to 20 million from Social Security alone.[3]

Still, our politics have reflected a continuing "yang" from the right ever since the "yin" of President Johnson. In 1991, the first President Bush chose the venue of a commencement address at the University of Michigan (where LBJ had made his Great Society speech in 1964) to contrast Johnson's Great Society with his own idea of a "good society." Bush characterized the Great Society as involving "huge and ambitious programs administered by the incumbent few." He declared that President Johnson had "believed that cadres of experts really could care for the millions and they would calculate ideal tax rates, ideal rates of expenditures on social programs, [and] ideal distributions of wealth and privilege." But, Bush continued, "No conclave of experts, no matter how brilliant, can match the sheer ingenuity of a market that collects and distributes the wisdoms of millions of people all pursuing their destinies in different ways."[4]

Johnson's actual remarks back in 1964 had been, however, quite different. In fact, poverty was not his sole or even his major focus, and big government was definitely not his solution. He had said, "The challenge of the next half century is whether we have the wisdom to use . . . [our] wealth to enrich and elevate our national life, and to advance the quality of our American civilization. . . .

[T]he Great Society is not a safe harbor, a resting place, a final objective, a finished work. It is a challenge constantly renewed, beckoning us toward a destiny where the meaning of our lives matches the marvelous products of our labor." After enumerating a series of problems needing national attention, including poverty as one item in a lengthy list, Johnson had concluded, "The solution to these problems does not rest on a massive program in Washington, nor can it rely solely on the strained resources of local authority. They require us to create new concepts of cooperation, a creative federalism, between the National Capital and the leaders of local communities." [5]

Bush's words decades later were just another stanza in the ever-echoing conservative refrain of failed big government. The conservative mantra since 1964 has been one of constant attack on big government and on assistance to low-income people (especially welfare) as promoting dependency. Their platform has stressed transfer of federal programs to the states with reduced funding and no accountability, privatization of the operation of publicly funded responsibilities such as corrections, application of market models generally, volunteerism, charity, and faith-based programs. And of course the so-called wars on crime and drugs have produced a rate of incarceration that tops the industrialized world and disproportionately chews up the lives of African American and Latino men.

Even with the Reagan budget cuts of the 1980s and the shifts in the economy that widened disparities in income, we ended up in the year 2000 in about the same place as we had been in 1973 as far as the national numbers on poverty and achieved progress on the overall numbers for poverty among minorities and single mothers with children. The outcomes have been more troubling with regard both to criminal justice and to welfare policy and in inner-city neighborhoods and rural and other high-poverty areas. And we are far from where we should be as a nation. The reasons why are a toxic pool of economic facts and nasty conservative politics, bubbling into the current of Republican resolve to defeat President Obama regardless of the damage it wreaks on the economy.

3

Why Are We Stuck?

The twenty-first century began with the nation in the best position on poverty in thirty years. At the end of the Clinton administration, the poverty level was 11.3 percent of the population, only a tick higher than the 1973 low point of 11.1 percent.[1] We weren't doing better, but we weren't doing worse.

Today, the situation is much worse, and not only because of the recession. Before the recession began, 6 million people were added to the ranks of the poor between 2000 and 2007. Another 9 million became poor between 2007 and 2010, the year when the total number of people in poverty reached 46.2 million, or 15.1 percent of the population. This was an increase of nearly 15 million since President Bill Clinton left office.[2] Family homelessness went up 20 percent between 2007 and 2010.[3]

The already grim news continued to worsen as I wrote this book in 2011. A study by the Pew Research Center confirmed that the current situation is more shocking than the numbers that relate only to income. The Pew Center reported that between 2005 and 2009 the median wealth of Hispanics fell by 66 percent and that of African Americans fell by 53 percent, while whites lost "only" a mere 16 percent. By 2009, the median wealth of white households was twenty times that of African Americans and eighteen times that of Latinos.[4] The damage caused by the housing bubble to people's savings and assets, including the disproportionate effect on minorities due to their having been targeted by predatory lenders, was intuitively obvious, but nonetheless the Pew documentation was stunning. (The Economic Policy Institute reported even more devastating figures, putting white median wealth at $97,860, 44.5 times that of African Americans. The absolute figure for black median household wealth was $2,200, down 65 percent since 1983.)

The Children's Defense Fund's annual report on the status of American children offered additional statistics. The number of children added to the rolls of the poor between 2008 and 2009 was the highest annual increase we have ever seen. The number of homeless children in public schools went up 41 percent in just that one year.[5] We are at a perilous place. Between the fragility of the economy and the fiscal and political facts in the public sector, it is hard to see when the numbers will improve. Nor is it clear what the future might hold thereafter.

My purpose in this chapter is to begin exploring why, despite the extensive efforts we have made in public policy, we did not make more progress on reducing poverty between 1973 and 2000. Before diving in, though, we need to understand better how we define poverty in the United States.

WHAT IS POVERTY?

Our American definition of poverty begins with Mollie Orshansky. For a middle-level bureaucrat in the Social Security Administration of five decades ago, she gets a lot of ink on Google. In a certain sphere, she actually is quite famous.

In the early 1960s, Orshansky had been doing her own research to develop a measure for poverty when word came down through the ranks officially assigning her (along with colleagues who remain less well known) to do the task. They set the cost of the economy food plan, the most modest diet as defined by the Department of Agriculture, as their cornerstone. Then, using data from a 1955 survey of consumer spending, they multiplied the cost of the minimal diet by three as an approximation of the remaining costs of an elemental living. Voila! The American poverty line. One suspects they might have thought that they should come up with a number on the low side so people wouldn't be too shocked. Adjusted for inflation, it is now about $18,000 for a family of three and a little more than $22,000 for a family of four.[6] Try living on that.

Besides being patently inadequate, the poverty measure we use is flawed in other ways. For one thing, it leaves out some categories of income. Income from cash benefits like Social Security, SSI, and welfare is included, but not in-kind benefits, so food stamps and housing vouchers (and a few other things) don't count as income. Also, it is pretax, so the effect of the Earned Income Tax Credit isn't taken into account. Not counting these items fuels the impression that nothing works, since a benefit seems to have no impact if we don't measure it. Of course, including these items would increase a person's income and therefore reduce the number of people counted as poor if in fact the current poverty line is set at the right level.

But it isn't. The other side of the ledger, the cost of living, is understated by the Orshansky methodology. A more accurate estimate of a survival cost of living dictates raising the poverty line. Experts estimate that the right multiplier of the basic diet today would be more than seven, not the three that Orshansky used (which probably was too low from the beginning).[7] The change in the multiplier is only a rough indicator: the cost of food has actually decreased relative to inflation, but the change does imply quite strongly that the poverty line we use now is too low. A full accounting for the real cost of a minimal living—including the costs of housing, food, clothing, utilities, energy, health care, child care, work expenses, and taxes—would be much more accurate and would also raise the poverty line and increase the number of people in poverty even when all sources of income are taken into account.

Much work by the National Academy of Sciences, the Census Bureau, and others has yielded a number of alternative poverty measures that are based on a percentage of actual consumer expenditures. They all result in somewhat higher poverty lines and raise the number of those living in poverty by about one to three percentage points, or roughly 3 to 9 million people.[8] Because they also include all sources of income and subtract such things as taxes, work and child care expenses, and out-of-pocket medical expenses, these alternative measures are a big step forward.

In November 2011, the government finally settled on one of the more modest of the alternatives as its Supplemental Poverty Measure (SPM). It concluded that the number of poor people in 2010 was 49.1 million, and the poverty rate was 16 percent.[9] This changes the distribution of the poor considerably. Because public benefits not previously counted raise a family's income, children show up as less poor than under the official measure. The elderly show up as poorer because they have significant out-of-pocket medical expenses that aren't taken into account by the official measure. One can argue that the SPM still understates the real cost of survival, but the more major point is that, with all public benefits now included in income, it is easy to see the impact that public benefits have in reducing poverty.

A completely different approach—not a measure of poverty—is to develop a full measure of families' basic needs. The Economic Policy Institute[10] and Wider Opportunities for Women[11] have found that a livable income is about twice the poverty line. This includes 103 million people at present and encompasses tens of millions who do not consider themselves poor. These initiatives are important instruments to inform public policy, but, for reasons of common sense as well as methodology, they are not an appropriate basis for measuring poverty.

The importance of looking at people with incomes below twice the poverty line is underscored by seeing what happens when the SPM is used. Under the new measure, the portion of the population with incomes below twice the poverty line rises to a remarkable 47.8 percent (or more than 146 million people), compared to the 34 percent (103 million people) who are below twice the poverty line under the official measure. A major reason why so many more people appear in this category is the cost of out-of-pocket medical expenses, which is becoming more and more burdensome. A second reason is that the effect of non-cash public benefits in raising incomes disappears at levels not much higher than the poverty line. Eligibility for most public benefits ends at income levels a little above the poverty line. The negative effect of out-of-pocket medical expenses will be ameliorated considerably when the Affordable Care Act becomes fully operative, but the SPM dramatically reveals how tenuous the position of the middle class is in our country.

HOW HAS THE PICTURE OF POVERTY CHANGED?

Poverty looks different now from the way it looked four decades ago. The elderly are much less poor, and children have become the poorest age group. Rural poverty, still somewhat on the high side percentage-wise, reflects many fewer people because fewer people now live in rural America—although those who do reside there are especially likely to be among the persistently poor. And suburban poverty has risen as older suburbs have become hospitable to large numbers of immigrants and to people moving from central cities. Suburban poverty grew 53 percent between 2000 and 2010, compared to "only" 16 percent in cities.[12]

What we have achieved for the elderly did not happen by accident and refutes accusations that poverty is intractable and that government policy does not work. Social Security payments were indexed to inflation in the early 1970s, and SSI was enacted. These two steps had a huge positive effect.

To understand why there is so much more poverty among children, we need to understand why their parents are worse off. The heart of the answer (at least when there are not extra millions of people out of work) is how pervasive low-wage work became beginning in the 1970s, coupled with the large increase in the number of single-parent families. Most of the income of low-income families comes from work,[13] but in jobs that either don't pay enough to get a family out of poverty or are available only part-time or seasonally—when the worker wants desperately to have

year-round, full-time employment. Many people work as hard as
they can but are still poor.

Many two-parent families have been able to cope with the plethora of low-wage jobs by sending a second adult — generally Mom —
out to work, but single mothers have no such option, and their
numbers were on the increase just when earning power stopped
growing forty years ago. So, interactively with the prevalence of low-
wage jobs, the increase in the number of female-headed families is
also a major factor in the stubbornness of poverty. Only 4 percent
of households with more than one earner are in poverty, compared
with 24 percent of households with a single earner.[14]

When it comes to the roles of race and gender in understanding
the narrative of poverty, there are two story lines, both important.

One, the largest number of the poor has always been white. The
crux of the poverty problem is often perceived as there being too
many African American single mothers. It is not: white is the pre-
dominant color of poverty. And the fact that the largest number of
the poor is white means that many of the remedies for poverty are
race- and gender-neutral and would benefit whites more than any
other group.

But two, poverty is still disproportionately present among people
of color and single mothers (and their children). That story line is
equally significant: African Americans, Latinos, and Native Americans are poor at close to three times the rate of whites. This disparity raises obvious questions of discrimination, both overt and more
subtle, embedded in the functioning of such systems as schools and
criminal justice.

So there are two narratives. The economic changes of the last
forty years hit all races, but these events hurt people of color extra hard. Economic mobility statistics make that point in dramatic
fashion: about 45 percent of African American children who lived
in middle-income families in 1968 ended up in the bottom fifth
of income earners as adults, compared to only 16 percent of white
children who started in middle-income circumstances at the same
time.[15] In other words, nearly half of African American children

who began their lives in middle-class circumstances when the economy began to sour landed in poverty (or near it) when they grew up, whereas just one in six whites were downwardly mobile.

Beyond all of these factors, many other forces cause poverty, are a result of it, exacerbate it, or all three, and the effects of many of these forces have increased over time. Poor education is a prime example, as is involvement in the criminal justice system or the foster care system. Disabilities and poor health, both physical and mental, are other cases in point; drug and alcohol abuse is another, as are child abuse and domestic violence.

So poverty has many faces. A family living in the *colonias* of South Texas faces challenges quite different from those of a family living in a high-poverty neighborhood in Chicago. An elderly widow with limited work history and no extended family has needs very different from an eighteen-year-old high school dropout looking for a job. A recovering alcoholic, an ex-offender, a chronic schizophrenic, and a victim of domestic violence each confront different barriers. The list is endless.

Another important dimension is the length of time people spend in poverty. Most people who experience poverty will do so for a short (or relatively short) period of time, but there is a significant minority—who are the object of negative judgments in some quarters—who remain persistently poor. Half of those in poverty in any given year will be there for only one year, and three-quarters will experience a spell of fewer than four years. Over the years, the number of people who will experience only a short period of poverty is quite large, and consequently a better safety net would substantially reduce the number in poverty at any given moment.

On the other hand, looking at how many people will be in continuing or recurrent poverty over ten years highlights the degree of persistent poverty. Slightly more than 44.1 percent of those who are poor on any given day will be poor for more than four years of the following ten. The figure for African Americans is 61 percent. The degree of persistent poverty speaks both to how much low-wage work we have and to the flimsiness of the safety net. In addition, persistent poverty appears disproportionately in places of concentrated poverty, locales where the problems are more complex and deeply ingrained and the necessary remedies much more multifaceted. I discuss this in a later chapter.

All of that said, the two biggest factors in the story of poverty over the past forty years are the changes in the American economy and the significant increase in the number of families headed by single mothers.

THE SUPER-RICH AND THE REST OF US

Conservative critics are quick to point out that we spend hundreds of billions of dollars every year to help low-income people and they remain in poverty. It must be their own fault, the critics say, or the policies must be wrong, or both.

But conservatives overlook one key fact: the American economy has changed radically over the past forty years. Wages have not risen and with that stagnation, the incomes of those in the bottom half have languished as well. Antipoverty remedies have been swimming upstream against these economic trends. Far more people would be poor without the remedies we have.

The economy has indeed grown, but the fruits of that growth have gone overwhelmingly to those at the top. The wealthy have gained spectacularly. The gap between the enriched top and the increasingly impoverished bottom (as well as that between the super-rich and the middle) is wider than ever.

There is little if any public awareness that half the jobs in the country pay less than $34,000 a year, and almost a quarter pay below the poverty line for a family of four ($22,000 a year). By one calculation, wages for the bottom half have risen less than 7 percent in real terms since 1973, less than a fifth of a percent a year.[16] By another—that of my colleague Harry Holzer, a labor economist—the increase has been a more substantial 22 percent, which is still considerably less than one percent annually. Either way, the wages for half the jobs in the country have basically stagnated. Large numbers of children have grown up to have jobs that pay less than what their parents earned. The number of people reporting that their current job was paying less than their previous job was 14 percent in 1991, and increased to 35 percent in 2010. The median real income of men aged thirty through thirty-nine actually decreased by 12.5 percent from 1974 to 2004. Only 31 percent of African Americans in the middle tier of income in 1968 earned more than their parents when they reached the age their parents were at that time.[17]

Meanwhile, the top 1 percent took in 9 percent of all personal income in 1979, and that figure skyrocketed to 23.5 percent in 2007. The top fifth took in 53 percent of all after-tax personal income in 2007.[18] The income of the top 1 percent went up a staggering 275 percent between 1979 and 2007, while that of the bottom 20 percent grew just 18 percent in those twenty-eight years.[19] (Income in the middle barely grew either.) The income of the top 0.1 percent (one one-thousandth of the population) increased a staggering 390 percent.

The widening of the wealth gap has been even more spectacular. The wealthiest 1 percent had 1,500 times more wealth than the bottom 40 percent in 1983, and this disparity widened to more than 4,400 by 2001.[20] By 2007, the top 1 percent held a larger share of income than at any time since 1928.[21]

If all those in the bottom half had livable incomes, we wouldn't need to be quite as concerned about the effect of the incomes of the super-rich on the rest of us. But as things are, the economic disparities in the United States are gross enough to have a moral dimension.

As I noted earlier, the number of people living in extreme poverty has shot up, especially during the past decade. The total was 12.6 million people in 2000, and grew to 20.5 million in 2010, constituting 6.7 percent of the population and 44.4 percent of the poor.[22] Nor is all of this simply a result of the recession. The number in extreme poverty had reached 15.6 million by 2007, before the recession had even begun.

We also don't hear much about people with incomes below twice the poverty line, which is approximately $36,000 for a family of three (or $44,000 for a family of four). Many studies conclude that this amount is the real level that we might define as "adequate"—the level at which a family can pay its routine bills every month, not have to count pennies before visiting a doctor or a dentist, or face a crisis due to unexpected costs like the need for a new furnace. The 103 million people who now live below that income level represent one in three Americans![23] It is certainly not appropriate to denominate all of these people as "poor," nor do they think of themselves in that way. But it is a very large number, and it surely has political implications that have not yet become a full-blown political issue. My explanation for this silence is that people blame themselves for not doing better or are at the least resigned to their fate, instead of realizing that the economy is structured so as to leave them in the lurch.

These two numbers—those living in extreme poverty and those living below twice the poverty line—are the consequence of both the economic and distributional history of the past four decades, and our failure to maintain a proper safety net, especially at the bottom. In fact, we have torn holes in the safety net we once had.

We have always claimed that we are a middle-class society, but let's be honest—that's not true for far too many people.

A LOW-WAGE ECONOMY

Except for the last half of the 1990s, the economic history of the past four decades has been one of near-stagnation for people with jobs that pay below the median wage—the entire bottom half. Understanding this history is vital to grasping why we have not made more progress in reducing poverty, but also why the income of all lower-income people has stagnated. It is all far more rooted in the prevalence of low-wage jobs and the ever-widening gap between rich and poor than we typically admit out loud. I'll talk more about this dichotomy in the next chapter.

Yet if we didn't have the public programs we have, poverty and hardship would be even more serious than they are.[24] Significant new federal funding over the decades kept the situations of the bottom half—especially families who would otherwise be in poverty or even facing destitution—from being as dire as they might have been. Nearly every program I mentioned earlier—food stamps, Medicaid, the Earned Income Tax Credit, and so on—has the effect, directly or indirectly, of adding to the income of lower-income families. These have been, and continue to be, wise investments to limit the damage done by the massive structural changes in our economy. As I said before, they kept something like 40 million people out of poverty in 2010. Of course, that fact doesn't stop the current Republican refrain that nearly half of Americans pay no federal income tax and ought to have "some skin in the game."

We do have good reason to worry about the future. In this globalized world, a serious question exists as to whether the fact that so many jobs in the United States pay such low wages is going to improve, no matter what we do. Despite how wealthy we are as a nation, further slippage in our global competitive position may reduce the availability of public funds to make up for the shortfall in wages, even assuming there is political support for spending the money—a mighty large assumption. Special interests and well-heeled individuals now more than ever rule the political roost, enabled further by the Supreme Court's pronouncement in its *Citizens United* decision that corporations have the same rights of free speech as do real people in the realm of campaign finance. Big business and the super-rich seem to have convinced the electorate to adopt an antitax position that covers the entire board and makes it much more difficult to see where the resources for increased public investment in low-income people would come from.

The only way we will improve the lot of the poor, stabilize the middle class, and protect our democracy is by requiring the rich to pay more of the cost (at minimum what they were paying before the Bush tax cuts) of governing the country that enables their huge accretion of wealth. There are other funding sources to meet national needs, beginning with responsible reductions in our bloated defense budget, which is greater than the defense budgets of the next seventeen countries combined,[25] but an augmented contribution from the wealthiest people is also needed. I do not believe in class warfare, but asking the rich to pay more is simply not class warfare: it is in their interest to do so. They benefit enormously from the stability of our system; they can't have appropriately educated workers without good schools; they won't have enough consumers for their products without paying their workers a decent wage. They should pay for what our society makes possible for them. That is part of bringing the budget toward balance. And it is a moral issue as well.

THE GROWTH IN THE NUMBER OF
FEMALE-HEADED FAMILIES

Regardless of the reasons, the growth in the number of female-headed families with children is a significant cause of the increase in child poverty. The combination of low-wage work with the changes in family composition has been highly detrimental. A family with only one wage-earner—especially a woman, who still earns 77 percent of what a man earns—is going to have a difficult time. And, although with many individual exceptions, the statistics leave no doubt that children of single parents—for economic reasons if nothing else—face longer odds for the future.

Working on issues of poverty in the mid-1960s, I saw the prospects for progress in the context of that era. We were still riding the wave of postwar prosperity despite the Vietnam War and the competition between guns and butter. We could still feel the wind of the civil rights movement at our back despite the civil unrest in our cities. We thought Richard Nixon was finished politically after he was defeated in his run for governor of California in 1962. To us, Watergate was merely a garish real estate development on the Potomac. The 1960s turned into a tough decade as it wore on, but we were still confident. Few, if any, foresaw the profound changes both in the economy and the structure of the American family that would greatly complicate the fight against poverty. I certainly did not.

Discussing such metamorphoses in the American family gets into muddy political waters, changes that have been sensationalized and used to blame the poor and especially women of color. But the changes are big and are important, and they do have major policy implications.

Between 1970 and 2009, the percentage of families headed by women with children under eighteen doubled—from 12.7 to 25.4 percent. The percentage of African American families with children that same age that were headed by women went from 37.1 percent in 1971 (the first year the statistics were broken down by race) to 52.7 percent in 2009. Most of these increases occurred during the 1970s, simultaneously with the wave of changes in the economy. The percentage of female-headed African American families had already climbed to 48.6 percent in 1980 and to 19.2 percent for all families.[26]

Reflecting these changes—and coupled with the increase in low-wage jobs and consequent difficulty for a single mother to support her family—the percentage of poor children under eighteen who lived in female-headed families rose from 24.1 in 1959 to 55 in 2010.

Paralleling the increase in the number of female-headed families has been the increase over the last seventy years in births to unmarried mothers of all races and ethnicities. The rate of births to unmarried women in the United States rose from under ten per thousand women in 1940 to more than fifty per thousand in 2006.[27] The changes cut across lines of race and ethnicity, although they occurred almost entirely among women who did not have a college degree.[28]

The pattern is similar across most of the developed world. From 1980 to 2007 in the United States, the percentage of births to unmarried women went from 18 to 40 percent. The UK's percentage went up much more, from 12 to 44 percent. The Netherlands went from 4 to 40 percent. France went from 11 to 50 percent. Iceland, with the highest numbers in both years, went from 40 to 66 percent. Japan went from 1 to 2 percent. In 2007, the United States ranked seventh out of fourteen countries examined by Stephanie Ventura of the National Bureau of Health Statistics and her co-authors,[29] which suggests that the changes were certainly not the unique result of American social policy. On the other hand, it should be noted that unmarried mothers in other countries are more likely to be living with the fathers of their children than is the case in the United States.

The numbers are much higher historically in the African American community, and consequently discussion of this issue has always had a racial component. But however surprising to some, the unmarried birth rate among African American women has actually decreased since 1970, from ninety-five per thousand women to seventy-two by 2006. White rates went from about fifteen per thousand women in 1970 to almost forty in 1998 (under thirty when Hispanics are counted separately). Unmarried birth rates among Hispanic women, counted separately since 1989, went from about 90 per thousand women to 106 in 2006.[30] Thus the growth in the rate of unmarried births in the United States over the past thirty years is almost entirely attributable to changes among whites and Hispanics.

The overall trend in teen out-of-wedlock births has been downward since 1991, when it was 61.8 per thousand. It hit 34.3 per thousand in 2010[31] and is now at the lowest level ever recorded, declining by 9 percent in 2010 alone. There were 409,840 teen births in 2009. Teenagers accounted for 23 percent of nonmarital births in 2007, down from 50 percent in 1970. The percentage drop since 1990 has been largest among African Americans, from one hundred per thousand unmarried African American teens to fifty-four per thousand in 2010.

Trends in the percentage of births that are out of wedlock are a significant and telling way to look at the problem. By 2007, 39.7 percent of all births were to unmarried women.[32] Again, this statistic shows that the increased incidence of nonmarital births cuts across lines of race and ethnicity, and should be a matter of concern regardless of race. Nonetheless, the percentage of births to unmarried African American women remains a particular concern. In 2009, 72.3 percent of African American children were born outside of marriage, compared to 24 percent in 1965. The trend among Hispanics was from 37 percent to 42 percent over the same period, and among whites was from 6 percent to 24 percent.[33]

Why the number of out-of-wedlock births was—and still is—so much higher in the African American community is not definitively answered by research. The allegation that low-income African American women have children in order to get on welfare or to get an increased welfare payment is hard to maintain in light of the declining level of welfare payments from the early 1970s onward. At the same time as births outside marriage were increasing, beginning in the 1970s, welfare benefits went down steadily relative to inflation in nearly all states.[34] And the increase in the benefit that came from having another child was in almost every state so small that it only threw the family into deeper poverty.

A partial explanation that makes sense to me is William Julius Wilson's "marriageable male" hypothesis, one which applies especially to people living in neighborhoods of concentrated poverty (including high-rise public housing).[35] Beginning in 1973, with deindustrialization occurring in the broader economy and affecting workers across the board, employment and wages of African American men, numbers which had been on the rise since 1945, took a nosedive; at the same time, the disproportionate incarceration of African American men began its steep climb. Women kept having children, but because the economic prospects of the children's fathers were so bleak, they did not marry.

One reason why so many African American women are coping on their own in raising their children is what the criminal justice system does to the men of the community, especially in the inner city. The massive and unnecessary imprisonment of African American men is preventing two-parent families from forming and destroying others on a large scale. Prison time takes away what could be productive and parental years by putting men behind bars with long sentences, and it jeopardizes the future because it blemishes their employment prospects so severely. In fact, poverty rates would be considerably higher if incarcerated men were counted for purposes of poverty, and ex-offenders with their high rates of unemployment drive up the current poverty number.

When compared to the trend since 2000, what happened in the late 1990s is particularly interesting. The last half of the 1990s was the only time since the early 1970s when there was noticeable real growth in both employment and real wages among lower-income families. Unmarried births declined among African American and Latino women during that period. That was also a time when welfare became less available due to the effects of the 1996 law. Some argue that the decline in unmarried births was due to the decline in the availability of welfare, whereas others credited the improved employment climate. The events of the past decade support the argument that variations in employment are the most important factor. Unmarried birth rates went up again during the middle of the past decade, but welfare did not become more available. The variables that did change were the availability of jobs and the level of wages.

Analysis of the research literature tells us that there is no clear explanation why unmarried birth rates among African Americans have historically been higher than those among whites, but the impaired economic situation of African American men since the mid-1970s is an especially noteworthy variable in the statistics.

Regardless of the explanation for the disparity, it is imperative that the issue be addressed. Conservatives say it is entirely a matter of personal responsibility. Some liberals seem to be in denial that there is actually an issue at all. But the consequences are undeniably troubling.[36]

The solutions are not simple. The aim is to postpone childbearing until the partners marry or establish a long-term commitment to each other and have a realistic economic approach to making it work. Hackneyed slogans, shibboleths, or bumper-sticker

simplicities will not suffice: improved educational and employment opportunities are critical, as are criminal justice reform and
strategies to build healthy neighborhoods. But programs at the
community level that stress postponing parenthood and that support responsible parenthood should it still occur are essential as
well, although granted, messages about the wisdom of delaying parenthood are more likely to be heeded in a world in which there are
viable escape routes out of poverty.

RACE AND GENDER

Issues of race and gender are at the heart of the public debate about
poverty. Such subjects are not new, but they appeared in new form
over the last four decades in the use of welfare and the criminal
justice system as race-related political issues.

The fact that the largest number of poor people are white is almost never mentioned. Ronald Reagan's fictional anecdote about
Cadillac-driving "welfare queens" pervades and pollutes our political culture. Everyone knew he was talking about African American
women. Millions of Americans instinctively associate "poverty"
with "black." This matters. The white majority is less likely to support safety-net programs if they think only or primarily blacks will
benefit.

Here resides the hot button. It is of course true that there is a
disproportionate number of African Americans and Latinos in poverty. The question is, "Why?" The debate divides, roughly speaking,
into two camps. One says the problem is basically structural: a pau-
city of good jobs, terrible schools, the cradle-to-prison pipeline that
disproportionately incarcerates poor minorities, race and gender
discrimination. The other postulates that the overriding problem
is with individual behavior and failure to take responsibility—
attributable to "bad parenting" and ensuing individual failure,
wrongheaded public policy, or both.

Because it is the image many have of American poverty in general, the continuing concentrated poverty in our inner cities is at

the heart of the debate. Comparatively speaking, the numbers for urban venues are not large, encompassing perhaps 10 to 12 percent of the poor.[37] But because these ghettos are even more disproportionately black and brown than poverty in general and because it is associated with media images of crime and children born to unmarried women, it shapes political debate and impedes efforts to craft broader solutions.

There is no question about the behaviors and the statistics. They include not only out-of-wedlock births and street crime, but also dropping out of school, gang violence and violence in the home, and drug and alcohol abuse, as well as the drug trade. The late senator Daniel Patrick Moynihan pointed to the "breakdown of the black family" in his famous (to many, infamous) report of 1965, eliciting a fusillade of unremitting flak. The result was that respected researchers steered a wide berth away from research on inner-city behaviors for more than two decades, until William Julius Wilson tackled the issue in his 1987 book *The Truly Disadvantaged*.

Wilson and others (including me) argue that the basic facts are the result of too many poor people all living in the same place— concentrated poverty. The increase in concentrated urban poverty resulted from the migration out of most middle-class residents, sparked by the unrest of the 1960s and the new protections against housing discrimination in the Fair Housing Act of 1968 and played out against the broader tableau of the growing scourge of low-wage work. Public policy, too, played a significant role, both in what it failed to do and what it did all too well. The failures were neglect of schools, lapses in helping people prepare for and find work, and lack of support for neighborhood-revitalization strategies. What public policy did all too well was to lock up the men of the community. What it did about welfare (before 1996) was a mixed bag. It did provide income to families that had no other source of support, but it failed to help (and push) recipients to get and keep jobs.

The new racialization of the politics of poverty coincided with the election of President Richard Nixon. He supported and signed important legislation expanding food stamps and creating housing vouchers and SSI, and also proposed a guaranteed minimum income. But, important as all these were, his overriding political focus concerning race was directed in a different direction, one that had significant implications for poverty.

The real focus of the Republican Party with regard to race inhered in its "southern strategy" to capture the South. The new political reality was that overtly antiracial policies like those of George Wallace and his ilk had become unacceptable. As a result, Republicans needed strategies that would communicate their racial slant without speaking in racial terms. Criminal justice and welfare were perfect vehicles.

The GOP appealed to white southerners (and others around the country) by advocating law enforcement policies that would disproportionately lock up black (and Latino) men and by harping on welfare. We have only to remember Reagan's "welfare queen" and the Willie Horton commercial that was run to discredit Governor Michael Dukakis during his presidential campaign against George H.W. Bush. (For those readers who don't remember or who weren't yet born, in 1988 Willie Horton absconded from a prison furlough in Massachusetts and committed assault, armed robbery, and rape. Lee Atwater, the brilliant political operative of then–vice president Bush, produced a political advertisement attacking Dukakis's furlough policy and showing Horton's picture. Horton was African American, and the racial message was not lost on voters: a vote for Dukakis would endorse not only being soft on crime but also a look-the-other-way posture toward the specter of violent black men preying on white communities. When Atwater was dying of brain cancer three years later, he apologized to Dukakis for the "naked cruelty" of the 1988 campaign.)

With regard to criminal justice, street crime, in fact, was on the rise, and it had a visible racial element. I was youth corrections commissioner in New York State in the mid- to late 1970s, and I saw it firsthand. My theory was that the containment of the inner-city unrest of the 1960s had plugged the outlets young people had for political protest, and that with no channels to express grievances, especially against the police, the continuing anger had erupted into sometimes-violent street crime.

As I noted earlier, the number of people receiving welfare benefits had increased greatly in the 1960s and become an important lifeline for inner-city mothers and children in the 1970s and thereafter. The increased presence of African American women and children on the welfare rolls served up juicy political fodder.

The response to street crime was to lock up African American and Latino men for longer and longer periods of time—including the thousands of men who committed low-level drug offenses— and to engage in the politics that went along with all of that. And it was clear that at every stage, from arrest through sentencing, African American and Latino men were (and still are) treated more harshly than were whites committing identical crimes.

The history of welfare is intertwined with that of criminal justice. The men were locked up, and the women subsisted on welfare. Attacks on welfare and tough rhetoric on crime were staples of Republican political campaigns from the 1970s on. Criminal justice policy changed greatly over those years, whereas welfare— though it was a favorite target for attack by President Reagan and also was the subject of numerous welfare-to-work initiatives at the state level in the 1980s, as well as a modest federal reform in 1988— had remained substantially unchanged when President Clinton took office in 1993. By then, there were 14.3 million people on welfare—disproportionately women of color and their children. With the changes in welfare embraced by Clinton, the rolls shrank to well under 5 million people, but most former recipients did not escape poverty. Single mothers who neither have a job nor receive welfare assistance now constitute, with their children, a substantial percentage of those in extreme poverty.[38]

The mantra of the right is, at best, simplistic. Single mothers, they say, should have jobs and/or get married. It is true that getting a job without getting married is possible for most people in good times, but even then, the problem is getting a job that at the very least gets the family out of poverty, especially if the woman has not graduated from high school (and, increasingly, even if she has). "So," the mantra continues, "they should get married." The point seems to be that then there will be two possible income-earners and everything will be hunky-dory.

We do want to make marriage more feasible. Children tend to do better when two parents are under one roof, and two wage-earners do make things easier, but it shouldn't be the case that the only route out of poverty is to get married to someone who also has a job. Jobs should pay enough so a single parent can support a family with two or three children on one job, a daunting challenge when a quarter of the jobs in the country pay less than $11 an hour. Single mothers work, in large numbers. The biggest problem is that the jobs don't pay enough to get them out of poverty. Besides, there is a rather serious problem of where to find a marriageable man. So many men are in jail or are ex-offenders who face almost insurmountable barriers to finding remunerative work. Marriage — which is a basic human instinct for most people — is not always achievable.

Welfare receded as a political issue after the 1996 law was enacted, but the hostility against it still lurks just below the surface. It is time to recognize the racialization of welfare and criminal justice policies for what they are doing to impede progress against poverty. The story of our economy and its negative effects on people of all races must take center stage, but the institutional racism embedded in our welfare, criminal justice, and education systems needs frontal attention as well if we are going to make real progress in reducing poverty and creating the kind of society we say we want.

4

Jobs:
The Economy and Public Policy Go South
(for Most of Us)

The heart of an antipoverty strategy is jobs—not just any job, but good jobs that bring with them enough income to live on and jobs that are at least ladders to jobs that pay a decent wage. And the heart of a strategy to create enough good jobs is a healthy economy, complemented by thoughtful public policy that maximizes workers' incomes. For most of the past forty years, the American economy has been successful in producing jobs but distressingly unsuccessful in producing jobs that lead to a livable income.

The largest single determinant of the twenty-first-century picture of poverty in America—putting aside the massive unemployment of the current recession—is the huge number of jobs we have that don't pay enough to live on.

In 1967, the Nobel Prize–winning economist James Tobin wrote an article in the *New Republic* titled "It Can Be Done! Conquering Poverty in the US by 1976."[1] His first claim was that "economic growth is still our most potent weapon."[2] There was more, including a proposal for an "incentive income supplement" to replace welfare that would have strengthened the safety net in times of recession.[3] But the heart of his optimism was an implicit confidence that the nation's economic growth would continue, and that with such growth would come the jobs that are the backbone of a nation with minimal poverty. Six years later, his prognostication still looked good: as noted earlier, the poverty rate declined to 11.1 percent in 1973.[4]

But potholes in the path of progress had also begun appearing. Industrial jobs, such as those in auto and steel plants, had been godsends for propelling the poorly educated sons of Appalachia and the Deep South into the middle class. But by 1973, many factories had moved south to get away from union wages. The nature of work was shifting toward jobs that required more skills. People without high school diplomas were more often coming up short in their efforts to find good jobs.

Politics were changing, too, and not just in regard to welfare and criminal justice. The election of President Nixon also brought to the fore an energized business community determined to dial down Washington's interference in their activities, a goal often antithetical to the interests of their workers. The Democrats still controlled Congress, but the suburbanization of the country was changing their profile and priorities (and southern Democrats still held the balance of power in Congress on many issues). Their core constituencies in the North and the West were still the unions (although not necessarily all union members) and minorities, but the battlegrounds—the places where they had to win to hold Senate seats and stay in the majority in the House—were shifting to the suburbs. A Democrat who wanted to win votes in the suburbs had to be for the environment, for good government, for the free market (with some regulation), for choice on abortion, for dovish foreign politics, and quite possibly against school busing and affirmative action.

THE 1973 OIL CRISIS

Nineteen seventy-three—the year of the first foreign oil shock—was a watershed year in the economy. The economic indicators that had been so consistently positive for nearly thirty years swerved into a sudden U-turn. Coincidental or not, one of the most telling changes in direction was the trend in wages for African American men with high school educations or less, wages that had risen steadily since 1945 but now swung in the opposite direction. The economy softened. Wages for those earning less than the median wage stagnated and—at the bottom—lost ground to inflation.

Wage growth in the bottom half of the labor market basically stopped. The median wage job paid $14.97 an hour in 1973 (in 2010 dollars), but increased only to $16.01 an hour in 2010, an increase of 6.9 percent over thirty-seven years, or less than 0.2 percent annually.[5] Things would have been even more grim but for the increase in real income during the tech boom in the last half of the 1990s.

The result is that half the jobs in the country pay less than $34,000 a year and a quarter pay less than the poverty line for a family of four. Families with two earners can do all right, but the large number of families with only one earner—typically a single mother—are in big trouble.

In retrospect, the 1970s were the run-up to the election of Ronald Reagan—the great turn to the right in post–New Deal politics that slammed the door shut on the New Deal era. Looking back, the signs had been accumulating. Jimmy Carter's presidency was the period of so-called stagflation: simultaneous high unemployment and high inflation, which was especially tough on people earning less than the median wage.[6] But that was just the beginning.

Other signs were in areas critically important to lower-income people. The unions in the private sector were losing power, and, not coincidentally, the minimum wage began losing ground relative to inflation.[7]

The trend in the overall economy was the great shrinkage—due to relentless global competition and technological change—in the availability of high-wage industrial jobs that didn't require extensive education and the increase of low-wage (mostly service) jobs in their stead. The new low-wage jobs included cleaning hotel rooms and homes, taking care of children, working in retail stores, serving fast food, emptying bedpans in hospitals, standing as security guards, and staffing consumer support lines—some of them involving tasks previously done at home by wives who were now in the labor market. Today, manufacturing reflects less than 10 percent of employment, down from 28 percent in 1960.[8]

As the nature of work changed, so, too, did the size and composition of the labor force. Women in large numbers sought employment, as did new immigrants, some in the country legally due to the historic 1965 immigration act but also some undocumented. Baby boomers joined the labor force in large numbers, too. The economy performed impressively in absorbing so many new entrants, but did badly regarding the remuneration of workers in the bottom half.

WHY DID WAGES STAY SO LOW?

The question is why were (and are) the wages at the lower end so low. Other countries experienced a loss of industrial jobs to less-developed countries and similar growth in poorly paying jobs, but they managed to mitigate these wage disparities better than the United States did. So why did it not happen here?

One big factor is what happened to unions. They began losing ground, both in organizing and in their political clout in Washington, D.C., and the states—ground they continue to lose to this day. Even during the Carter years, with sixty-one Democrats in the Senate (as well as some "moderate Republicans," a political breed now extinct) and a large majority in the House, the unions were unable to break a Senate filibuster of a bill that would have made it easier to organize, despite the fact that it was their major objective and was strongly backed by the president.[9] President Carter also proposed to index the minimum wage to the average wage for manufacturing employees, but he lost on that, too.[10] The National Labor Relations Board (NLRB) could not keep up with the volume of complaints about the ubiquitous union-busting tactics by businesses the unions were trying to organize, particularly since employers fought every complaint vigorously. And once President

Reagan was elected, he filled the Labor Board with antiunion appointees who turned a completely deaf ear to such complaints.

To some extent, unions were victims of their own success. Some factory workers, now middle class, had moved to the suburbs and accordingly thought they didn't need a union any more. Some lifelong Democrats even migrated to the Republican side; others, still staunch unionists, voted first for George Wallace for president and then turned Republican because of their anger over school busing and affirmative action, despite knowing that Republican and prounion tenets were increasingly contradictory.

Overall, unions lost ground for three reasons: employer opposition and weaker laws, structural changes in the economy toward white-collar work and largely decentralized services and away from sectors where unions were historically strong, and more product and labor market competition around the world.[11] Unions have more trouble thriving in a world in which industries are no longer organized as stable clusters of a few big firms with large profits to share. When unionized companies face nonunionized competitors, whether at home or abroad, increases in labor costs can no longer be passed on to the consumer. Increased competition through international trade and deregulation made it more difficult for unionized companies to continue to prosper.[12]

An important chapter in the story of union decline centers on the resurgent political activity of the corporate world in the 1970s, activity that came along in a most timely way to finance the rising cost of political campaigns and elect pro-business candidates. This swing was coupled with changes in the attitude of the electorate — not only the suburbanization of the Democratic Party but also the enhanced power of Sunbelt states due to migration and the political awakening of evangelical Christians after *Roe v. Wade*. In other countries — France being one example — unions are not overwhelming in their numbers but nonetheless have broad public support. The changes in voter attitudes in the United States are surely a factor in the decline of unions.

So the political losses of the unions were not accidents, and corporate interests did spend large sums of money lobbying for the other side. Nor was this renewed activity of big business fortuitous. The year 1970 had seen a wave of labor unrest second only to that of 1946 in postwar years: 2.4 million workers out on strike for extended periods, thirty-four strikes involving more than ten thousand workers, and a slew of slowdowns and wildcat strikes.[13] Inspired by the civil rights movement and the 1960s inclination to "question authority," there was a new restlessness among younger workers, who rebelled against their sclerotic leadership and sought democracy within their unions. This trend was as threatening to business as it was to the union leadership. By the time Jimmy Carter took office, the new political vigor of big business had taken hold, along with continuing globalization and the alteration of the economy, and the die was cast against the unions.

The numbers are well known. Unions represented 31.8 percent of the labor force in 1948.[14] By 2010, they represented a mere 11.9 percent.[15] The demise of unions has been especially significant in the private sector. Private-sector union membership was 24.5 percent in 1973, 16.5 percent in 1983, 11.1 percent in 1992, and only 6.9 percent in 2006.[16]

If the weakening of unions in fact did play a big role in the growth of wage inequality in the United States, we would expect to see greater disparity in wages in the United States compared to those in countries with stronger unions. That is exactly the case. In a 1996 study, Cornell economists Francine Blau and Lawrence Kahn looked at seven countries and discovered that the wage differential between workers in the fiftieth percentile and those in the bottom tenth percentile in the United States was larger than in any of the other countries they examined. The UK was the only other country that had experienced decreases in union membership comparable to those in the United States, and it saw a similar growth in wage disparity.[17]

The campaign against unions continues to this day, taking the form now of virulent attacks on public-employee unions. Now even the public-sector unions—the last vestige of strong union membership—are feeling the pressure from politicians whose campaigns are heavily funded by corporate money. Not satisfied with the atrophy of unions in the private sector, the new wave of right-wing Republican governors paints public employees as caricatures of the Mandarin elite, with deliciously early retirement opportunities and gilt-edged pensions, all achieved by overreaching unions that are soaking taxpayers. Witness Wisconsin governor Scott Walker, who acted to take away state employees' right to collective bargaining even after the unions offered heavy concessions. And add to the antiunion list Ohio governor John Kasich and New Jersey governor Chris Christie.

Nor are these governors the only attackers. The radical right House of Representatives has passed legislation—virtually overnight, with no debate—to eviscerate the NLRB. That legislation will not survive in the current Senate, but the House will meanwhile pursue its agenda by slashing the NLRB's appropriation—a strategy that may have considerable success in a world of budget-cutting where the only action is in the zero-sum area of domestic discretionary spending.

The weakness of the minimum wage was a second major factor. UC Berkeley economist David Card and Princeton economist (and, as of 2011, chair of President Obama's Council of Economic Advisers) Alan Krueger estimate that 20 to 30 percent of the rise in wage inequality in this country can be attributed to the decline in the real value of the minimum wage.[18] When it was first enacted during the New Deal, the minimum wage was set at a level that was half the average wage. The current $7.25 minimum wage was just 39 percent of the average wage in 2010. If the original minimum wage had kept pace with the increases in the average wage, it would have risen to $9.30 in 2010.

There is a long-standing argument among economists about whether raising the minimum wage destroys jobs. Pathbreaking work by Card and Krueger in the 1990s suggested that reasonable increases in the minimum wage do not have any negative effect on jobs.[19] Arguing the other side, UC Irvine economist David Neumark posits that the bulk of the research conducted since 1990 shows minimum-wage increases have a negative employment effect on low-skilled workers.[20] Needless to say, Card and Krueger and many others disagree. In a different category from Neumark are the arguments of people whose views are simply ideological. Alan Greenspan, for example, told Congress in 2001 that, were he able, he would abolish the minimum wage, because it is "artificial government intervention" that hurts jobs.[21]

Putting Greenspan's extremist views aside, a reasonable reading of the research supports continued strengthening of the minimum wage. It is true that, in today's globalized world, employers can more easily eliminate jobs when costs rise, although it's also the case that a large share of minimum-wage jobs are in service sectors that are not involved in global competition and cannot be replaced by technology. Consider home health care. My instinct has always been that any minimum-wage increase that is politically feasible is not one that would have negative economic effects. In any case, the weakening of the minimum wage is part of the story of the weakening of wage levels at the bottom.

A third factor was the flood of new entrants into the workforce beginning in the 1970s because of immigration, of the babyboomers coming of age, and especially because of the large numbers of women who decided to work outside the home. That these groups found jobs in large numbers—albeit in disproportionately low-wage work—was remarkable, particularly in light of the fact that so many industrial jobs were being lost at that time.

Women went from constituting 35.3 percent of the workforce in 1969 to 49.9 percent in 2009, the year when women constituted half of all workers for the first time.[22] The percentage of women with children under six who were working in 1975 was 39.6; in 2008 it was 64.3.[23] Four in ten mothers are now the sole or higher-earning breadwinners in the home.[24]

Women's wages went up overall, but many women in low-wage work did not fare better. Remember that close to half of all female-headed families with children live in poverty. Single mothers are far more likely than are women in general to have low-wage jobs. Nor is child support playing the role it should be in filling the gap. Only 42 percent of custodial mothers are receiving child support from their children's fathers, and fewer than half of those receive the full payments ordered.[25] These numbers have improved over the past few years, but we have a long way to go.

Immigration and trade have played a role, too. The question about immigration is not whether it had an effect on wages at the lower end, but whether the effect was significant. Between 1970 and 1996, the population of foreign-born people in the United States increased by 15 million. Arriving immigrants have less schooling than does the average American, and that gap has been ever increasing, so it is not surprising that these immigrants are more concentrated in low-skill jobs,[26] although the overall composition is becoming bimodal as more and more higher-skilled workers have been entering the country. Nonetheless, Harvard economist George J. Borjas and his co-authors, who earlier estimated that immigration had only a modest effect on wage disparities between 1980 and 1995,[27] concluded in a later study that subsequent immigration did harm the employment opportunities of competing native workers.[28] On the other hand, David Card, using a different methodology, contends that immigration has not had a significant negative effect.[29]

There are obviously two quite separable issues here: legal immigrants and undocumented workers. It stands to reason that all immigration of low-skilled workers, because it expands the labor supply, will tend to depress wages. Nonetheless, reams of research conclude that our current legal immigration policy is on the whole a plus, all things considered. The broader question concerns undocumented workers. Our policy has been totally hypocritical. On one side, we express horror at the number of people here illegally, but until recently we have taken practically no steps to prevent employers from hiring and then exploiting undocumented workers. We have been like a schizophrenic police officer who purports to stop traffic with one hand but waves it along with the other. This

is unacceptable. It has produced inhumane treatment of undocumented workers by employers—dangerous working conditions; il-
legal pay levels; and, all too often, total dereliction of pay. We have
enabled employers to hire people at a significantly lower cost than
what they would have to pay citizens and legal immigrants. The oft-
repeated declaration that these are jobs no one else would take is
a gross distortion, although it is quite likely that no one else would
accept a job on the exploitative and often dangerous terms imposed
on undocumented workers. If the employers had to obey the law,
most would still find workers—with the possible exception of back-
breaking tasks such as farm work—even when there is no recession.
It is just that they would have to pay more. Our policy should include a path to citizenship for those undocumented people already
here, an effective policy at the border, and humane enforcement
of immigration laws. At the same time, we need to find a way to pe-
nalize employers for hiring people in the country illegally without
permitting discrimination against others—primarily Latino—who
are citizens or are here legally.

Trade has had a clear impact on jobs. Whatever the facts were
prior to the 1990s, NAFTA and other trade agreements have had a
visible effect on jobs. There is substantial merit to the widely held
view that such agreements should have had stronger guarantees
of fair labor standards and environmental protections. Adherents
of this view argue that fewer jobs in the United States would have
been lost if such standards and protections had been insisted upon
and implemented.

A somewhat different question, however, is how these agreements affected low-wage sectors specifically in terms of destroying
jobs and lowering wages. The most recent research indicates that
increased trade affects jobs at all levels. Labor economists David
Autor, David Dorn, and Gordon H. Hanson found that, between
1991 and 2000, increased trade with China accounted for 19 percent of the decline in American manufacturing jobs in that decade,
and a stunning 32 percent of the decline between 2000 and 2007.[30]
The entry of China into the World Trade Organization and the

concomitant awarding of "most favored nation" status to China, as well as admitting China without regulatory standards, have had major impacts on American jobs. So have China's blatant currency manipulations to keep the dollar high and the yuan low.

Some economists ascribe quite a different set of reasons for the weakness of wage growth in the bottom half of the labor market— "skill-biased technological change theory" (SBTC). Their basic argument is that technological change and a dearth of skilled workers precipitated what happened in the labor market. Computerization and the spread of information technology required more highly skilled workers, those who could command a wage premium. But, the argument goes, a sufficient supply of such workers was not forthcoming, a shortfall that left an overabundance of workers at the bottom. So, they conclude, the imbalance resulted in a bidding-up of wages on the top end and a pushing down of wages at the bottom.

The core of the argument is the idea that we missed a great opportunity by failing to educate and properly train enough workers—a supply-side failure, in effect. The story has some merit but recounts only a part of what transpired. Harvard economists Claudia Goldin and Lawrence Katz argue persuasively that, had educational attainment improved in the later 1970s and 1980s at the same pace as it had earlier, the demand side of the labor market would have adjusted to the larger supply of skills by generating more skilled jobs, albeit perhaps at a somewhat lower wage. Goldin and Katz and others believe that employers over the longer run will hire more skilled workers if there is a larger supply of skilled applicants. Employers claim, even now, that they have skilled jobs going begging in areas like nursing, engineering of various kinds, and such trades as electrical work because they cannot find qualified workers.[31]

The question, nonetheless, is how much weight to give the SBTC argument in explaining the overall outcomes for wages. An enormous number of lower-wage workers saw their wages barely go up or even decline over the past forty years. Given the number of low-wage workers, a mismatch between new, more technologically complex jobs and the number of workers available to fill them can at best be only part of the explanation for why the incomes of tens of millions of people stagnated or worse.

The SBTC hypothesis has driven policy arguments that are only part of what we need to focus on. SBTC proponents argue that education differences are the prime driver of inequality and that educational improvement therefore has to be a central policy focus at all levels of government. President George W. Bush's treasury secretary, Henry M. Paulson, said, "[T]hose workers with less education and fewer skills will realize fewer rewards and have fewer opportunities to advance."[32]

This is true, as far as it goes. Improvement of education is a must, and every person should pursue as much education as will maximize his or her economic prospects. Paulson pointed out that "in 2004, workers with a bachelor's degree earned almost $23,000 more per year, on average, than workers with a high school degree only."[33] So of course everyone who has the ability to obtain a four-year degree should have the opportunity to get one.

But what works on an individual level is not the full answer for society as a whole. We have to focus as well on the number of "good" jobs that are available for people who go to the effort of getting a college degree or some equivalent postsecondary training. Declaring to everyone that getting a college education will fix everything is only half-true: the graduates have to be able to get a job after they graduate—not to mention to be able to afford that college education in the first place. Those who argue that extending postsecondary education to far larger numbers of people will solve the entire problem are shilling a modern form of patent medicine.

If we are to create an economy in which people are able to earn a livable income, we must answer four basic questions: (1) What can we do to increase the number of better jobs? (2) What can we do to increase the pay for the jobs we have? (3) What can we do if—after we do everything possible to raise wages for the jobs we have—the labor market still fails and jobs still do not pay enough to live on? and (4) What can we do to restore a more equitable distribution of income and wealth?

CAN WE HOPE FOR BETTER JOBS?

The first step to better jobs is a sensible and coherent national macroeconomic policy. The current impasse in our politics stands in the way of a full-employment approach. We have to move toward aligning our spending and our revenues, but one would not know from much of the political discourse in Washington that we still have an unacceptable number of people — 15 million — out of work. Our policy should be geared in the short run to helping people get back to work. We should also legislate now to repair our fiscal future, with the plan to go into effect when the economy is on a stronger footing. But we should act immediately to bring big business and wealthy people back to the tax rates they paid in the 1990s when the economy boomed — and from which, by the way, they profited quite nicely. As things are, the naysayers are burying our national head in the sand.

In the short run, we missed a bet in 2009 in the design of the stimulus, and we are still missing the bet as recovery of jobs continues at an excruciatingly slow pace (although what we should be doing is no longer a political possibility). We should have learned a lesson from the New Deal and put 2 million people to work in twenty-first-century versions of the Civilian Conservation Corps and the Works Progress Administration. Having 2 million people working at important tasks and sporting distinctive shirts and caps would have created a visible national response to the recession. We could have enlisted state and local government in the effort so that it could be implemented quickly. The money earned by the participants would have begun circulating in the economy with a multiplier effect.

President Franklin D. Roosevelt's job-creation programs spanned the period from 1933 until shortly after World War II began. They began with the Civilian Conservations Corps, which put people to

work in the national parks and forests, and the Civil Works Administration, which grew quickly to more than 4 million workers and
contracted into the Federal Emergency Relief Administration a few
months later, in the spring of 1934. The more lasting initiative was
the Works Progress Administration (WPA), which FDR presented
as the centerpiece of his State of the Union address in 1935. The
WPA was an expansive effort, with one division constructing important and attractive public works and public buildings that are
still in use, and many other projects, including a variety of activities
engaging artists, writers, musicians, and actors—even a circus. It
employed as many as 2.8 million people over the extended period
of its existence.[34]

In August 2011, Illinois representative Jan Schakowsky introduced the Emergency Jobs to Restore the American Dream Act,
which would create more than 2 million new jobs over two years
doing things we need to have done: 650,000 jobs building and
maintaining schools; 100,000 jobs for young people to replicate the
New Deal Civilian Conservation Corps; 250,000 work-study jobs to
help college students put themselves through college; 350,000 jobs
for laid-off teachers, police officers, and firefighters; 40,000 health
care jobs for underserved areas; and 750,000 green jobs in weatherization, housing construction, and other tasks.

I don't expect Schakowsky's bill will be enacted by the time this
book is published. I do understand she probably knows that, but
that's not the point. The point is that her bill was the right thing to
do. Something like it should have been enacted in 2009 and is still
needed now, sad to say.

For the longer run, one thing we need is to expand AmeriCorps
and make it an avenue to the labor market for the huge number of
young people who face a rocky road to steady work. AmeriCorps
can also build civic values for participants of all backgrounds. It
is important to remember that when the New Deal made retirement possible by enacting Social Security and removed children
from the labor market by prohibiting child labor, it also reduced
the number of people competing for jobs in a terrible labor market.

Investing more in national and community service and making a strong effort to recruit low-income young people would now, among other things, have a similar effect in tightening the labor market. Nor will the problem with employment opportunities for job seekers in their late teens and early twenties end when the recession is truly over. We need to make the case for a much greater public investment in giving young people a chance to serve their communities and at the same time gather momentum toward more education and steady work.

The bigger question, of course, is about jobs in the private sector.

Looking at Bureau of Labor Statistics (BLS) projections for job growth in the coming years is an occasion for further gloom: fifteen of the top thirty job categories and seven of the top ten are rated by BLS as either low-wage or very low-wage. Four of the top ten are very low-wage—home health aides, food preparation and service workers, personal and home care aides, and retail salespersons. The only categories of better jobs in the top ten are registered nurses, accountants and auditors, and postsecondary teachers—although those three are in fact rated very high.[35]

My colleague Harry Holzer is less gloomy in his jobs forecast than I am. He has studied what he calls "middle-skill" jobs and finds hope there. To begin with, he rejects the argument that there is a "hollowing of the middle" going on which will result in an "hourglass economy." He says that middle-skill jobs represented about 55 percent of all jobs in 1986 and—while they did decline over the ensuing years—in 2006, they still represented 48 percent of all jobs.

Middle-skill jobs, according to Holzer, cut across many sectors and pay from $40,000 to $70,000 annually. He includes many health care positions; skilled crafts in construction; skilled workers in manufacturing such as machinists and welders; technicians in equipment installation and repair jobs that will result from a shift to a "greener" economy; police officers and firefighters; and a variety of positions in the service sector such as legal aides, protective service employees, and cooks and chefs in restaurants. He states that "a wide range of evidence shows that employers often have difficulty filling these . . . jobs."[36]

Holzer points to projections of increases in the number of middle-skill jobs and notes, importantly, that there will also be a significant number of openings created by baby boomers who will retire in the coming years. He does not deny that there will still be too high a percentage of low-wage jobs; his main assertion is that middle-skill jobs are an important category of work that will be available to young people of all backgrounds who pursue the education and training necessary to qualify for them. He emphasizes particularly the requirement of postsecondary education and training that these jobs entail—not necessarily a bachelor's degree but postsecondary education and training broadly defined. I'll talk more in a later chapter about what we need to do to provide the proper educational pathways.

I should also say a few words about "green jobs." Green jobs are being touted by some as a major component of the future job picture. The premise is that our national good sense will lead us to make the public and associated private investments necessary to wean us away from our dependencies on foreign oil and fossil fuels regardless of their origin and to create a fully sustainable environment for our children. Doing so, proponents say, will create an impressive array of new jobs. Yes?

Maybe, but the prospects look much dimmer now than they did in the euphoric first days after President Obama's inauguration. The first question, obviously, is whether we will have both the sense and the political will to make the necessary investments. If so, the investments will create jobs, although they will also destroy jobs in those energy sectors no longer favored. The second question is whether all the jobs will be good jobs—jobs that will support a family. And the third (of special concern here) is whether the jobs, insofar as they are good jobs, will be accessible to low-income young people just starting out and older people who are currently stuck in a low-wage rut.

Green jobs exist now across the economy. They include people who design, build, and retrofit homes and buildings; others who operate, maintain, and conserve all manner of "green" things; and still others who do the related business tasks of sales and customer service and accounting. They encompass employment in renewable energy and energy efficiency, construction, weatherization, clean transportation, environmentally friendly production, natural resource conservation, pollution mitigation and control, and sustainable agriculture. Some of the jobs are in "clean" areas such as solar and wind power, and others are in traditional areas that are becoming "green," such as building construction and manufacturing processes.

Studies project that anywhere from 4 million to 16 million new green jobs will come on line over the next two decades,[37] although many green jobs that had been expected to appear in the United States have shown up in China and Japan instead. Anything in the neighborhood of that higher number will be achieved only through public investment that leverages private investment, and only through a great deal of political will. Green industries will require subsidies and tax incentives, preferences in public procurement, loan guarantees to leverage private investment, and higher energy prices. Strong environmental regulation restricting carbon-based emissions, air and water pollutants, and solid and hazardous waste, as well as mandates for the use of renewable energy by utilities and minimum recycled content in some manufactured goods will be necessary, too.

Green jobs adherents profess full awareness of the challenges involved in ensuring that the jobs pay enough to live on. Effective labor standards will be needed. Subsidies and tax expenditures should be accompanied by requirements that workers be paid the prevailing wage. And energy-efficiency standards for appliances and other products should incorporate standards on wages and working conditions.

Civic partnerships at the local level will be especially important to delivering a fair share of the jobs to lower-income people, especially young people finding their ways into the job market. Proper education and training, delivered broadly, requires cooperation among schools, community colleges, community organizations, unions, and public agencies. Employers need to be involved in designing both the training and the process of placement. A strong partnership among all of these actors will be important in pulling together the required education and training funds.

Green jobs are a twenty-first-century idea. Their reality in scale and their relevance to lower-income people are still in question, but there is enough potential to warrant discussion in a chapter that discusses where the good jobs are going to be established.

Besides the macroeconomic policies we pursue to revive the economy, and beyond specific steps we take to create green jobs or other industrial policies to increase the number of jobs in the economy, we also need policies to see that the jobs we have are equally accessible to all. One thing this means is stronger enforcement of all applicable antidiscrimination laws. Another is to facilitate entry into the labor market for people who face particular barriers: the disabled, young people at the margins of inclusion, welfare recipients, ex-offenders, and the homeless, to describe a few. Of course, strong labor markets break down some of the barriers on their own, as they did in the late 1990s. So the bigger question is having enough good jobs, but the issue of equal access to the jobs we do have has been a challenge for a long time and still is.

CAN WE INCREASE THE PAY FOR
THE JOBS WE HAVE?

Yes we can, to borrow a phrase. Raising the minimum wage should be a primary objective both nationally and at the state and local levels. Equally important is seeing to it that the laws we already have on the books are enforced. Wage theft is ubiquitous and comes in a dizzying array of forms. Beginning with simply not paying wages that are owed, there are literally dozens of different schemes. Some are even allowed by current law, but they all abuse workers unconscionably. Revitalizing union efficacy would make an enormous difference, too, although how to make that happen is no simple matter.

The Minimum Wage

Last increased in 2006, the federal minimum wage is currently $7.25 an hour. A full-time, year-round minimum-wage job yields an income of $15,080—about $3,000 less than the poverty line for a family of three and more than $7,000 less than the poverty level for a family of four. When it was enacted, a decade after the previous increase, it came fairly close to the poverty line for a family of three, but even at today's low inflation rate it is gradually falling back again. Raising it to $10 an hour, an amount that would put it roughly in line with that of 1968, would yield an annual income of $20,800—still below the poverty line for a family of four.

Would such an increase have an unduly negative effect on jobs? The research I cited earlier would suggest not (although that view is not unanimous). The minimum wage can and should be increased to a more adequate level. But, vitally important as the minimum wage is, it only makes a dent in achieving what our goal should be. And that is to raise incomes to a level of basic adequacy, or twice the poverty line—a level higher than the current individual earnings of 44 percent of working-age adults in this country.[38] Other measures will therefore be needed to raise incomes beyond the level of the minimum wage, as I'll discuss later in this chapter.

Also, the minimum wage and other labor laws still leave out some groups. The Fair Labor Standards Act (FLSA) is still interpreted to exclude home care workers from both minimum wage and overtime protections, although as of January 2012 a new Department of Labor regulation to rectify this is pending. The FLSA also excludes agricultural workers from overtime. Domestic workers are not covered by federal job-safety laws or overtime pay requirements. Nor does the National Labor Relations Act accord the right to organize to agricultural workers or domestic workers.[39] When I went with Robert Kennedy to meet César Chávez in 1966, I don't think any of the three of us thought that such a hole in the law would still be there nearly half a century later.

The federal minimum wage does not operate in a vacuum. Seventeen states and the District of Columbia—generally jurisdictions with higher costs of living—have minimum wages higher than the federal minimum. Only five have no minimum wage of their own. State minimum-wage laws are still important targets for improvement, but what advocates and organizers accomplished with the state minimum wage during the past decade is an important case study, particularly because it is an example of successful advocacy by unions in partnership with others.

The federal minimum wage was stuck during the Gingrich years at $5.15 an hour and was steadily losing ground to inflation. The Service Employees International Union, along with other unions and some faith-based and community groups, decided to pursue change at the state level through legislation and ballot initiatives. Campaigns to raise the state minimum wage were successful in Oregon, Washington, and California, and were followed in 2004 by spectacular successes in Florida and Nevada, ones that included annual cost-of-living increases and engaged low-income voters in the process.

These successes led to plans in 2006 for ballot initiatives in eight more states, and merely the threat of such a campaign led the legislatures in Michigan and Arkansas to raise the minimum wage by statute and thereby head off a possible skew toward Democratic candidates if there was a ballot measure that would draw low-income voters. These remarkable state changes played a major role in paving the way for the federal increase to $7.25. By 2007, thirty-three states had raised their minimum wages—some to levels more than 50 percent higher than the federal minimum wage. The number with levels higher than the federal level went from ten in 1999 to seventeen (plus D.C.) at present.

Governments have other points of leverage on wages, too. A recent study reported that employees of federal contractors are paid less than federal workers—20 percent of contractors' workers are paid less than the poverty line for a family of four, compared to 8 percent of the government's own employees. States offering tax incentives to entice businesses to relocate could require that they pay their employees a decent wage, as some already do. Reimbursement regimens in health care could also require that nursing homes and home health agencies pay wages above the poverty line.

Dozens of local governments require a "living wage" for employees of businesses to which they award contracts for services or tax abatements for development projects. They typically require a wage of $10 an hour with benefits and $11.50 without. Critics claim that such laws deter economic development or hurt employment, but a recent Center for American Progress study of fifteen cities with living-wage laws found the same levels of employment growth as in similar cities without such requirements.

Wage Theft

The all-too-real world of low-wage work is sordid beyond belief and has worsened with the flood of undocumented workers. The most heinous of those involved are the employers who just plain cheat their workers out of pay and blatantly flout health and safety rules. Dishwashers, office cleaners, day laborers, nannies, health care aides, packinghouse workers, and sweatshop factory employees by the millions in cities and towns across America endure this reality every day. If employers don't outright withhold overtime or even a basic paycheck, they evade the law by using subcontractors and pretending not to know what is going on under their noses, or classify their employees as independent contractors and thereby shirk their own responsibilities. Unlawful deductions from wages and off-the-clock work are common. Chicago organizer Kim Bobo's excellent book *Wage Theft in America* lays out the issues in stark terms.

Researchers surveyed workers in Chicago, Los Angeles, and New York and learned that in just the previous week 26 percent had not been paid the minimum wage and 76 percent had not been paid for overtime.[40] A national survey in 2006 found that at least once in the previous two months, half of all day laborers received no compensation at all. A study of New York City restaurant workers in 2005 found 13 percent had not been paid the minimum wage and 60 percent were neither compensated for overtime nor received required rest breaks. In Massachusetts, from 1995 to 2003, misclassification of workers as independent contractors jumped from 8 percent to 19 percent.[41]

The amount of money being stolen from workers is astronomical. The study in Chicago, New York, and Los Angeles concluded that workers in those three cities lose an average of $56.4 million every week because of law violations.[42] Annualized, we're talking about $2.5 billion *in just those three cities.*

Workers are scared to file complaints for fear they will be fired or, if in the country illegally, deported. Law-abiding employers feel pressure to cheat and thereby not lose business to shady competitors. Enforcement agencies are woefully understaffed, and, depending on which party is in power, they fail to use even the limited capacity they have. The Government Accountability Office reports that enforcement actions by the Department of Labor's Wage and Hour Division dropped by more than a third from 1997 to 2007, a fact not unrelated to which party was in power for most of that period.[43]

The Obama administration added about 250 inspectors to the Wage and Hour Division, bringing the total number to nine hundred.[44] The states contribute about six hundred more inspectors to the mix. But with 8 million workplaces to cover, the challenge is still daunting, to say the least.

Still, there is much that can be done. The National Employment Law Project (NELP) and dozens of other advocacy organizations, including unions such as the Service Employees International Union (SEIU), have come together in a Just Pay Working Group to strategize and act. They are working with the Labor Department to target high-violation industries and—rather than waiting for individual complaints—consult with outside groups that are knowledgeable about the situations on the ground.[45] NELP has also published a lengthy advocates' policy guide on wage theft that offers more than two dozen suggestions for state and local legislation.

The states of Colorado, Illinois, Maine, Maryland, New Mexico, New York, and Washington have all toughened laws against wage theft, embodying recommendations of the Just Pay Working Group and NELP. All were the result of organizing and advocacy by unions, faith-based groups, and sundry other allies. During the summer of 2011, San Francisco enacted a Wage Theft Prevention Ordinance that was the result of a campaign led by the Progressive Workers Alliance, a coalition spearheaded by Interfaith Workers Alliance, the Chicago-based organization headed by Kim Bobo that works closely with NELP and SEIU. The ordinance embodies many of the provisions in the NELP policy guide: doubled retaliation penalties, penalties for not posting minimum-wage notices, a requirement that employers notify employees of a pending investigation, and a mandate that all cases be resolved within one year.

Unions

If there is a silver lining in the current mess, it is that perhaps it will get people to see the importance of banding together to protect themselves. Nonetheless, the prospects for broad-scale union revitalization in the immediate future look pretty dim.

The unions need labor law reform in order to have a reasonable shot at neutralizing the effective advantages employers have when unions try to organize. Currently, employers can get away with firing organizers among their employees and with stalling contract negotiations almost ad infinitum even when a union is successful in winning an organizing vote. Most important to the unions is the Employee Free Choice Act legislation, which would reform the way in which elections are conducted. They were unable to get such legislation when Carter and Clinton were president, and their quest gave way to other administration priorities during the first two years of the Obama administration.[46] Having a Democratic majority, even sixty votes in the Senate, doesn't mean there is a super-majority or even a simple majority when it comes to labor law reform. If that fact doesn't speak volumes about the state of our politics and about who holds sway, I don't know what can.

I do not mean to paint a picture that is wholly bleak. Unions— some of them, anyway—are still an important progressive force. The state minimum-wage story and the current work on wage theft are only two recent examples of important changes in which unions have played a major role. These examples suggest the possibility of a European model of a more general-purpose political and social advocacy role for unions to pursue on behalf of their members.

HOW DO WE RAISE INCOMES IF JOBS STILL DON'T PAY ENOUGH TO LIVE ON?

Here's the situation. Surprising as it may be, we do not have—nor are we going to have any time soon—enough good jobs for all people to earn a decent income. In 2010, 103 million people in this rich country had incomes that did not ensure their regular ability to pay for such essentials as food, housing, and health care, much less accumulate any savings—incomes of less than twice the poverty line, or less than $44,000 for a family of four.

The minimum wage, raised to the maximum that is possible politically, cannot get us to where we need to be. Unions, fully revived, will not get us there either. We have become a low-wage nation. "Bipolar," one might say, where those at the top have absconded with all the fruits of economic growth over the past forty years and continue to feather their nest even when millions of people are in deep trouble. A well-functioning economy in a prosperous nation surely ought to produce jobs that pay a living wage to every worker.

There has to be something else—actually, more than one something else. Fortunately, we do have some policies that work. They don't close the income gap, but they do make a big difference in people's lives.

These measures come in two categories: one directly raises the incomes of low-wage workers, mainly parents in families with children; the other is what I call "matters of societal responsibility" that also have the effect of adding to incomes. These include health coverage, assistance with the cost of housing, child care, and postsecondary education.

The federal Earned Income Tax Credit (EITC) is the leading income supplement. It is a great policy and a political success, at least up to now. It's what is called a refundable tax credit. "Refundable" means that the government writes a check to the taxpayer, who otherwise owes no federal income tax or owes less than the amount of the credit.

The benefit increases each year to keep up with inflation. In 2011, the EITC added a maximum of $5,112 to the annual income of a minimum-wage worker with two children, an amount that gets a family of that size with a minimum-wage job out of poverty.[47] (There is also a three-child category, enacted on a temporary basis in President Obama's Recovery Act.) With one child, the maximum is $3,094. Single individuals qualify for the EITC as well, but with a maximum payment of only $464.[48]

The EITC was enacted in 1975 and has been substantially expanded over the years, especially in 1993 on the initiative of President Clinton, but also including major expansions in 1986 and 1990—all with bipartisan support. It is a powerful tool, lifting more than 4 million people out of poverty. Its cost is now well over $40 billion, and it has a very high participation rate—well over 80 percent of those eligible.[49]

The EITC is not perfect. It contains a marriage penalty that is still a challenge to policy makers. For example, if two single parents, each with one child and receiving the EITC, marry each other, their EITC payment will decrease. Combining two households that have two children each could cut the total EITC in half.

Another important issue relates to single individuals, or at least to noncustodial parents.[50] The current supplement to the income of single individuals is a maximum of $464, as I noted earlier. Raising that figure would reduce somewhat the poverty of unmarried low-income workers, of whom there are millions, and also would help low-income noncustodial parents fulfill child support obligations that they cannot meet at present.

One reason the EITC has been a political success is because employers like it. It frees them from paying more out of their own pockets in wages. To put it bluntly, that's not so great. It probably makes it more difficult to pass increases in minimum wages. The minimum wage and the EITC have to remain in continuous tension with each other. We require an EITC because wages are so low, but, to minimize the free ride the EITC is giving to some employers, we need to keep improving the minimum wage. Employer support for the EITC has not stopped some right-wing politicians from attacking it for letting too many people escape from having to pay federal income taxes, but the simple truth is that if workers had more income, they would pay federal income taxes.

Twenty-two states have EITCs as well. So do the District of Columbia (to me, a state); New York City; and Montgomery County, Maryland. They range from Louisiana's modest provision of a refundable state tax credit at 3.5 percent of the federal EITC up to a 35 percent refundable credit in the District of Columbia, although most are being cut badly in the recession-driven fiscal crisis. This is fertile ground for more work once state coffers recover from the current crises.

Another effective income supplement is the Child Tax Credit (CTC). This is a $1,000-per-child tax credit (subtraction from taxes) for people who pay taxes, but it is also refundable for those with low incomes. Currently, a family needs $3,000 of income before it receives a payment. For each dollar a household with children earns over $3,000, it receives a 15-cent CTC payment.[51] So, for example, a mother of two children with an income of $13,000 receives a payment of $1,500, 15 percent of $10,000. This amount is over and above what she receives under the EITC. The Center on Budget and Policy Priorities estimates that the refundable portion of the credit reaches 13 million people and keeps 2.3 million out of poverty at an annual cost of about $5 billion. But the

$3,000 threshold is a temporary antirecessionary measure. If it is not renewed by the end of 2012, the income threshold for eligibility will revert to a prerecession level of about $13,000, and the impact will shrink by about 90 percent.

The three-child EITC category and the $3,000 threshold for the CTC, added as temporary provisions in the Recovery Act, were originally slated to expire at the end of 2011. In the great tax "compromise" at the end of 2010 that kept the Bush tax cuts for rich people in effect, one of the fig leaves was to extend the EITC and CTC provisions for another year.

Although these income supplements are doing a reasonable job in raising many low-wage workers out of poverty, we would need to do much more to reach everyone whose income leaves them short of having enough to live on.

The UK during the Blair-Brown period accomplished much more than we did in the United States in using tax policy to increase incentives to work. The UK Working Tax Credit was similar to our EITC, but there was a child care component that was worth almost $15,000 for families with one child and $25,400 for families with two or more children.[52]

Let us turn to category number two, where reside the things that a caring nation sees as its social responsibility to provide, either universally and free or on a means-tested basis. In this category I include health care, child care, housing, and education from prekindergarten through college. The glass that holds category number two has filled substantially thanks to Obama. Sixteen million or more people will be added to Medicaid under his health care legislation.[53] A somewhat strange gap in Medicaid over its nearly half-century of operation is that it omitted most low-income adults from coverage (except for the elderly and the disabled). Only the parents in welfare families were covered and these were mainly women; even these women constituted only a small fraction of the population of low-income women. All poor children are already covered under Medicaid, and the combination of Medicare and

Medicaid takes care of the elderly and the disabled, but other adults were mainly out of luck. What Obama has accomplished is truly historic.

Medicaid coverage for people with incomes below 133 percent of the poverty line will effectively supplement wages for workers (and add income for others), as will subsidized coverage for somewhat higher-wage workers who purchase health insurance through the exchanges that will be set up under the law.

Another income equivalent that needs to be strengthened is child care. During World War II, the government subsidized child care to enable women to work in the war plants. Called the Lanham Act, its funding disappeared after the war when women were no longer urgently needed (or, some would say, wanted) for work outside the home.

Federal funding specifically for child care did not reappear until 1988, culminating a twenty-year debate that was highly politicized and acrimonious. President Nixon vetoed comprehensive child care legislation passed by the Democratic Congress in 1971, calling it "a communal approach to child rearing over against the family-centered approach."[54] Nixon had just returned from his historic trip to China and wanted to do something to assuage right-wing critics of his journey. For nearly two decades thereafter, extreme conservatives blocked significant federal funding for child care. The logjam was broken during the presidencies of Ronald Reagan and George H.W. Bush, who, in contrast to Nixon, signed bills focused specifically on child care enacted by Democratic Congresses.

The federal role was expanded somewhat in conjunction with the 1996 welfare law. The idea was that if mothers of small children were going to be pushed into the job market, child care should be available. Perhaps not surprisingly, the level of funding has not been consonant with the rhetoric, especially since there is no legal right to assistance. Over the past fifteen years, federal funding for child care has been essentially level, meeting the needs of approximately one in seven mothers who are income-eligible for assistance.[55] Child care assistance for all who need it in order to work outside the home is critical if mothers are going to succeed in the workplace. And, again, it is an item that has monetary value — one that effectively adds to the low-wage worker's income.

The third vital income equivalent is housing. Housing is a major component in the cost of living for low-income people, and it has become more and more expensive in recent years. The generally accepted rule of thumb is that housing should constitute no more than 30 percent of a family's budget. By this standard, more than half of all renters lived in unaffordable housing in 2009, and 7.1 million households either paid more than 50 percent of their income in rent or lived in severely substandard rental housing, a 20 percent increase just from 2007 (probably due more to falling incomes than rising rents).[56] According to federal guidelines, there is not one state in which a family with one minimum-wage job can afford to rent a two-bedroom home or apartment at the federally defined "fair market rent" for that state.[57]

The two major federal policies in this area are public housing and housing vouchers. Federally financed public housing, which goes back to the New Deal, has an inventory of about 1.2 million units. Housing vouchers, enacted in the Nixon era, serve more than 2 million families. Together, the two programs reach about one in four people out of the population whose incomes would qualify them for participation if sufficient funding existed. For those low-income people who are fortunate enough to have it, help with housing is a major supplement to income.

The fourth major income equivalent we have is help with postsecondary education, mainly Pell Grants. Named for Senator Claiborne Pell of Rhode Island, the grants are another Nixon-era creation. They are now ample enough to pay community-college tuition in most states, although students still need to find other ways to pay for the other costs of daily life, which can be a tall order, and the limited grant size precludes many from attending a four-year college. Another problem now is that there are not enough community-college seats, and for-profit colleges have entered the arena. These profit-making entities pose a serious problem. Too many have troublingly low graduation rates, and some offer programs that are so grossly inadequate as to border on fraud. Some are outright scams. A mountain of evidence tells us that they need to be regulated much more closely, the claims of their well-paid lobbyists to the contrary notwithstanding.

I said it earlier, but it bears repeating that because of all these programs we have many fewer poor people, and millions of low-wage workers are better off. If housing and child care reached everyone who needs help, even more low-wage workers would be closer to a living income. It would be wonderful if all workers were paid enough so that we didn't need to subsidize things like child care and housing. Unfortunately, that's not the America we live in.

Increasing the income of low-wage workers, by whatever means, would be good economic policy, too. As President Franklin Roosevelt once succinctly remarked, "Cheap wages mean low buying power."

HOW CAN WE ACHIEVE A MORE EQUITABLE DISTRIBUTION OF INCOME AND WEALTH?

This is the 64-gazillion-dollar question, but history does provide hope. The rich have always had too much power in our country, but the extent of that power has waxed and waned. Sometimes the people have pushed back and won. The voracity of the railroads, the oil companies, and other industries in the late nineteenth century created a populist rebellion, which in turn resulted in the Interstate Commerce Act and the Sherman Antitrust Act. What followed was the Progressive Era, during which a coalition of immigrant workers, muckraking journalists, urban reformers, and followers of the social gospel produced both a sharper backlash against corporate power and a new spate of socially oriented legislation. And of course the Depression gave us the New Deal and the broad support for the historic laws enacted through the leadership of FDR.

We have been moving to the right for a long time. The path from Nixon to Reagan to Gingrich to George W. Bush (and particularly Dick Cheney) and, more recently, on to the Tea Party is truly frightening. Each Republican ascendancy in our political cycles has been farther to the right than the one before. Civil rights sent much of the South into Republican hands. Vietnam and Watergate tore a hole in our national confidence in government. *Roe v. Wade* energized the socially conservative right. Free-flowing campaign contributions powered the machine of the corporate right. And Democrats are seen by a wide slice of the electorate as not having held up their side of the bargain. Large numbers of the currently disaffected see both parties as having done little over the years to alleviate the ever-increasing economic squeeze on the lower half (or maybe the lower 55 or 60 percent—pick your number). So, if government doesn't help regular people, why strengthen government? Why have a government at all? Might as well vote for the party that wants to shrink the government to the point where it can be drowned in a bathtub.

And now? What is happening now makes Nixon and even Reagan look (to some) like moderates. Bad times evoke anger—more easily if that ire has been simmering for a long time. In our deeply divided country the Tea Party has power far beyond its actual numbers. The weak economy plays into the long-accumulating loss of popular confidence in government solutions. Obama is seen by many as having helped Wall Street more than Main Street (a sentiment shared by people on the left as well as on the right, but with different conclusions as to what should be done). Many of those who do want to tax the rich want to send the proceeds to reduce the accumulated national debt rather than help people in need, even the victims of the recession. (And I have to say, many people still do not accept the idea of an African American president.)

I am far from the first to suggest that there is a cynical alliance between the rich and powerful and the socially conservative and economically angry voters who are among those injured by the behavior of the rich and powerful. But there is just such an alliance, implicit though it may be, and it is all too successful. The non-rich portion of the alliance participates because of their disillusionment with or downright hatred of government (and, in better times, because of their social conservatism). But someone might ask why the rich and powerful would oppose measures to help lower-income people—what difference does it make to them? The answer is that more than anything they want low taxes (and no regulation), and it is harder to maintain low taxes if government is going to spend money to help people who do need it (and take care of things such as health care that help many people who are not poor). No doubt some understand that money in ordinary people's pockets creates demand for corporate products over the longer term, but corporate horizons are nothing if not short-term. Selfishness trumps selflessness.

Politically, the few remaining Republicans with moderate records are terrified of primary opponents from the Tea Party, and they act accordingly. Senators with long records of bipartisan cooperation on many key issues now vote most of the time as though they never saw a constructive proposal from the Democratic side. The politics of the moment exacerbates the substantive impasse.

Current politics will not change until a sufficient bloc of voters gets sufficiently disgusted to take action. Obama, running for reelection, needs to make the challenge to the powerful the centerpiece of his campaign. He began to do that with speeches at the end of 2011 as I wrote these words, and such leadership in pressing the issue, if it continues, will pull it toward the front burner.

But people must not be passive. It has been astonishing to me that so many people who have been hurt badly by the recession and Washington's failure to build on the stimulus package of 2009 have been so silent. The only noise has come from the right, which in its anger and frustration has come to include many people who have decided, often against their own economic interest, that government is useless (except for defense and law enforcement). The president will be more likely to continue his emphasis on the obligation of the rich to pay more if more people vocalize their support for his doing so and press him to do so if he falters.

As of the end of 2011, many of us are watching with sympathetic interest the course of the Occupy Wall Street movement around the country and wondering what seeds it will sow. As I write, the encampment phase seems to be winding down, but the idea of "We are the 99%" has begun to sprout more widely. Occupy Wall Street has definitely vaulted issues of inequality to a higher position in public consciousness, and there is a sharp increase in the media coverage of inequality. The big question is whether the Occupy effort will inspire and create space for a broader coalition that will gather political momentum. That is the real hope.

But beyond the as-yet-unanswered questions, it is also not clear whether the aims of "the 99%" actually include the whole 99 percent. Getting the rich and business to pay more in taxes than their secretaries is critical, but it isn't necessarily the beginning of a better politics about poverty or even the 103 million people with incomes below twice the poverty line. If we are going to make headway, leadership from the top and action from the bottom must coalesce. Can it be done? At the very least, there is one fact that points toward an affirmative answer: the self-aggrandizement of the super-rich is in its own way as dangerous to our democracy as the atrocities of the robber barons of more than a century ago.

5

Deep Poverty:
A Gigantic Hole in the Safety Net

An agenda to attack poverty divides itself into the here and now and the future—in essence, what needs to be done about jobs and income in the present and what we need to do to invest in children. The here-and-now part divides again, into remedying the weakness of the labor market and weaving a much sturdier safety net. The American safety net is much more fragmented than that of every other industrialized country, and its biggest hole is its deterioration with regard to the utterly destitute. And the question arises now about whether our entire safety net needs to be redefined. Low-wage work is here to stay, and it appears we are in for an exceptionally prolonged period of high unemployment. These developments imply a need for fundamental changes in policy.

All of that said, we are not without measures that lift people out of deep poverty, which is my particular focus in this chapter. Remember that the traditional measure of poverty doesn't count in-kind income (e.g., food stamps and housing vouchers) and is done on a before-tax basis (so it also doesn't count the EITC), although it does count TANF, Social Security, and SSI, which are paid in cash. So we have to be aware that the conventional measure overstates to some extent the number—to remind, 20.5 million in 2010—who are counted as extremely poor.

What does that mean in practice? Arloc Sherman of the Center on Budget and Policy Priorities has analyzed the impact of public benefits in reducing deep poverty. The good news is they do indeed reduce the incidence of deep poverty. The bad news is twofold. One, the effect of these policies on people in extreme poverty, almost invariably, is to raise them up only to "regular" poverty, not to lift them out of poverty altogether. And two, there are still something like 15 million people in deep poverty instead of the 20.5 million shown by the census, even after all public benefits are taken into account.[1]

Using the National Academy of Sciences alternative poverty line, which takes all forms of cash and cash-equivalent income into account, Sherman found that food stamps are the most powerful antidote for deep poverty. In 2005, food stamps raised 1.6 million children out of deep poverty. Social Security was second, lifting about 800,000 children—mainly children of deceased workers—out of deep poverty. Next, SSI raised some 700,000 children out of deep poverty who were either disabled or had a disabled parent. TANF and EITC each removed about 600,000 children from poverty, and housing assistance helped about half a million escape.[2]

Even when all the benefits are taken into account, the trend is bad. Sherman calculated that deep poverty among children rose nearly 75 percent from 1995 to 2005, and it had risen another 30 percent by 2010.

Why the rise since the mid-1990s? The biggest reason is the near-demise of welfare. The 1996 law ended the legal right to cash assistance and imposed a five-year lifetime limit on federally financed help to any given family. States responded to their newfound discretion with gusto, reducing welfare rolls nationally by two-thirds in just a few years. Such discretion was not only accompanied by a strong message from Washington to get people off the rolls, but also by a substantial fiscal incentive. Each state receives a fixed amount of federal funds regardless of the size of its rolls, so reducing the rolls frees up funds that can be used for other purposes.

Sherman points out that, in 1995, Aid to Families with Dependent Children (AFDC), the predecessor to TANF, raised from extreme poverty to "regular" poverty 62 percent of the children whose families would otherwise have had incomes that low. In contrast, by 2005, TANF was lifting just 21 percent of children out of what would otherwise have been deep poverty. In Sherman's words, "The number of children shielded from deep poverty by TANF cash assistance dropped by 1.6 million—from 2.2 million in 1995 to 645,000 in 2005."

Who are these extremely poor Americans? For one thing, they live disproportionately in the South, where rural joblessness and poorly paid seasonal work are endemic and TANF benefits are very low, assisting only small percentages of those who should be eligible. Eleven of the fifteen states with the highest rates of deep poverty are in that region, and 42.2 percent of all who are in deep poverty live there (although the South has just 36 percent of the nation's population). Half of all African Americans who are extremely poor live in the South (and African Americans are extremely poor at a rate more than double the general population). Of those children who live in deep poverty, 76 percent are in single-parent households.[3]

One piece of relatively good news is that people tend not to be mired permanently in deep poverty. Common sense tells us this, since it is hard to see how a family would survive for the long term if its income never exceeded half the poverty line (although there are such families). What little data we have suggests that half the extremely poor get out of deep poverty after a year (although they may well have other spells down the road). Of people with incomes below half the poverty line, only one in four is deeply poor three years in a row. For children especially, this is cold comfort. Even six months of the kind of trauma that deep poverty entails can derail a child emotionally, psychologically, physically, and educationally for a much longer period. Even a short spell among the deeply poor can have lingering effects that harm a person or family for much longer than the basic statistics would indicate.

One reason why families may not show up in deep poverty for very long is that they tend to break up. The children are sent to live with relatives or are taken away by the state. Parents make desperate choices such as prostitution and land in jail or in the morgue. And the problem may actually be understated because such people are homeless or otherwise unreachable by sampling interviews.

All of this raises a rather important question. If the need for safety-net support for those at the very bottom—at least to keep them from the most severe privation—is quite temporary for most, why not respond to it? Helping them would not cost much and would be hard for conservatives to attack as an incentive for people not to help themselves. Of course, the need to help them out of "regular" poverty would remain.

So why don't we act? I think one part of the answer, although not the whole answer, is that the vast majority of Americans are utterly unaware of the shocking fact that I mentioned earlier—that we have 6 million people whose only income comes from food stamps, Jason DeParle's great journalism notwithstanding.

WHAT HAPPENED TO WELFARE?

Whatever else was true about the welfare system we had before 1996, the safety net it provided for mothers and children with very low incomes, along with food stamps, afforded protection against utter destitution. That is gone now in many states. In Wyoming, for example, there were 318 families—644 people altogether—in the entire state receiving TANF in September 2010, about 4 percent of the state's poor children.[4]

What happened? How did TANF come to be?

Welfare has never been popular. Franklin Roosevelt called "a continued dependence on relief . . . a narcotic, a subtle destroyer of the human spirit." Robert Kennedy said that welfare was "degrading, both to the giver and the recipient." Kennedy's point, much like Roosevelt's, was that we had "ignored the real need—which was, and remains, decent, dignified jobs for all."

There *was* something wrong with welfare when Bill Clinton took office as president. I'm sure Robert Kennedy would have thought so, and I'm quite certain Franklin Roosevelt would have as well. (I thought so, too.) The portion of our population receiving AFDC was more than 5 percent—one out of twenty people—the highest it had ever been. Something *was* wrong.

Two things were wrong—one substantive and the other political—but what we did in response to them had terrible results. Speaking to the merits, welfare had never contained a serious jobs policy. That was what Kennedy was complaining about, and it was still true when Clinton took office. There were 14 million–plus people on welfare—5 million adults, mostly mothers, and their children—because no one had ever made a serious effort (which would have cost more money than letting them stay on welfare) to do what was necessary to help them get and hold on to jobs. There had been a positive, albeit modest, effort with the Family Support Act of 1988, but the states, coping with a recession as the law came on line, did not put up their share of the funding, and the law was effectively washed away. Recessions are never a good time to put people to work unless the government creates the jobs.

Welfare *should* mainly be a residual idea—a last resort for people who have no other recourse. For the most part, it should be temporary, and in fact—again, despite what conservative dogma would have you believe—it was always the case that the vast majority of recipients had short stays on the rolls. The anger that boiled up politically in the late 1980s and early 1990s came in response not only to the size of the rolls, but also to the discovery that even though most recipients left welfare quickly, about half of those on the rolls on any given day had been there for a long time. (How could both of these statements be true? Picture a hospital with two beds: one has ten people in it over a ten-day period, one person per day; the other has the same person in it all ten days. Ten out of eleven people are in the hospital for one day, but on any given day, half the population is there for a long stay. The point is the same as the one I made earlier about persistent poverty.)

The correct answer to the substantive problem—albeit one that would have cost some money—was to make the serious effort on the jobs front that no one had ever made. But the politics pointed in a different direction. The big rise in the welfare rolls in the 1960s engendered an unremitting attack on welfare, heavily driven by race politics. The election of Reagan brought leadership for the anti-welfare campaign to the White House. There *were* too many people on welfare, but it was never a fiscal drain. It never amounted to more than 1 percent of the federal budget. But, egged on by the multi-decade right-wing attack on welfare, voters were angry that a substantial number of individuals who could and should be working for a living, as they saw it, were getting something for nothing.

Candidate Clinton, dogged by issues about his personal life, ran head-on into the issue in New Hampshire, where the powerful archconservative Manchester *Union Leader* newspaper was stoking the fire. Well-versed on the issue from his national leadership on the 1988 law, he responded by saying he would "end welfare as we know it," thereby burnishing his credentials as a "new" Democrat and going on to a strong showing in the state's primary that revived his candidacy.

As president, Clinton pursued health care initially and offered a welfare bill in 1994 that proposed a largely incremental set of reforms. But the new Republican congressional majority elected that fall brought the issue to center stage by saying, in effect, "End welfare as we know it? We know how to do that."

Clinton signaled in the fall of 1995 that he would sign a bill making fundamental changes along the lines the Republicans were pushing, but then vetoed two versions the Republicans figured he would not accept, although the second was quite close to the version he ultimately signed. For the next six months, their political strategy was to blame Clinton for not signing a bill. In June 1996, however, they decided to try again. Fearing they had no accomplishments to take to the voters after two years in control and thinking (correctly) that Clinton, with the election looming, would sign a radical reform bill, they sent him a bill much like the one he had vetoed in January. This time, in August 1996, he signed it.

The consequence was the quintessential example of Clinton's penchant for triangulation. By signing the bill he helped (as he saw it) to ensure his own reelection but also helped the Republicans retain control of Congress.

The meaning for low-income people was an end to the statutory entitlement to cash assistance, replacing it with a block grant giving states wide discretion as to whom they would help and how, and installing a five-year lifetime time limit on the use of federal funds to assist any particular family.

I should say a word about my personal involvement in this history. I was Assistant Secretary for Planning and Evaluation at the Department of Health and Human Services when TANF was enacted, and I resigned my position in protest. I wrote an article in *The Atlantic* spelling out the consequences that I believed would ensue, and for that I have since become a minor character in the narrative that extols the wonderful success of TANF. The largely Republican references to me in the story make fun of the dire predictions I made about the spike in child poverty the law would bring about. I am sorry to have to say that I was correct. The worst consequences did not ensue during the first few years after the law passed because of the hot economy of the time (which no one foresaw). Even so, 40 percent of the women who left welfare during that period ended up without either a job or cash assistance, and nearly half of those ended up without any other support mechanism—without getting married, getting SSI, or moving in with family. The damage done by TANF has become even clearer in the last decade, culminating in its near-uselessness during the current recession. Of course, all of this doesn't stop the political narrative about TANF's great success from continuing to be told without amendment, just as it doesn't stop conservatives from continuing to say that people are still having babies in order to get welfare even though there is effectively no welfare to get in most states.

WHAT DID TANF DO?

AFDC was hardly generous, but it did reach a significant proportion of poor families. The level of benefits was always set by the state, but the law required that states provide benefits to everyone defined as eligible by federal and state law—an "entitlement," which has become an epithet in the political world.

The combination of AFDC and food stamps provided an income of about 60 percent of the poverty line in the median state, with the range being from 40 percent in the lowest-paying state (always Mississippi, where the AFDC benefit was—and TANF still is—about 12 percent of the poverty line), up to around 80 percent in the highest-paying cluster of states. Like TANF benefits today, AFDC benefits were not indexed to rises in the cost of living and consequently lost more than 40 percent of their purchasing power between the early 1970s and the mid-1990s. (TANF has lost 28 percent of its value since it was enacted in 1996 because its $16.6 billion annual appropriation has never been increased, but the huge decreases in the number of recipients left every state with plenty of funding to keep benefit levels current with inflation or even increase benefits if they chose to do so.)

Because AFDC was an entitlement, participation rates were fairly high—around 80 percent of those eligible and 60-plus percent of all poor children. (Under both AFDC and now TANF, states set the income levels to qualify for benefits, which are typically well below the poverty line.) So there was something of a safety net for families with children. The percentages of participation now are about half what they were before TANF was enacted in 1996: about 40 percent of those eligible and well under 30 percent of all poor children.[5] There were always people in deep poverty, but nothing—not even close—to what we have now.

The erosion goes well beyond what inflation did to the already-inadequate benefit levels, which were never generous and were downright stingy in many states. The spectacular changes have been in the levels of participation—not surprising since the number of recipients hovers around 4 million in the whole country after being more than 14 million prior to the enactment of TANF.

The Wyoming number I mentioned earlier is not an anomaly. In nineteen states, 20 percent or fewer of poor families with children received TANF in 2008. In eleven states, 12 percent or fewer were getting TANF. The six worst states were Wyoming, Idaho, Texas, Louisiana, Illinois, and Oklahoma.[6]

The best state for reaching poor families was California, at 73 percent, far more than any other state, although it has cut back its program substantially in the fiscal carnage of the last three years—and, paradoxically, has an especially bad record of reaching those eligible for food stamps. The only state even close on TANF was Massachusetts, at 67 percent. The rest of the states serving 50 percent or more of their poor families with children were Maine, Rhode Island, Washington, and Connecticut. California had 30 percent of all the TANF recipients in the country in 2008, although that figure is probably smaller now.

The states with low benefits generally (but not uniformly) coincided with those that served low percentages of their poverty population. Benefit levels were less than half the poverty line in every state. Thirty states offered benefits below 30 percent of the poverty line. Thirteen provided benefits at less than 20 percent of the poverty line. The lowest, at 15 percent of the poverty line or less, were Mississippi, Tennessee, Arkansas, and Alabama. South Carolina joined this dismal group in 2011, cutting its benefits to 14 percent of the poverty line.

In Mississippi, for the 11 percent of poor families with children lucky enough to get welfare, the combination of welfare and food stamps yields an income that measures a little over 40 percent of the poverty line. In other words, even a family receiving both TANF and SNAP is living in deep poverty in the state of Mississippi, or less than $9,000 for a family of three.

The "high" benefit states—with TANF benefits measuring above 40 percent of poverty—were Alaska (50 percent); California (49 percent); New York (47 percent); Vermont (44 percent); and Massachusetts, Wisconsin, and New Hampshire (each at 43 percent). Keep in mind that food stamps have to be factored in to understand what the safety net is in each state, and also that food stamp allotments are reduced by about thirty cents for every dollar of earnings or cash assistance. Thus, even in the high-benefit states, a family whose only income comes from TANF and SNAP is getting an income at less than 70 percent of the poverty line—enough to avoid extreme poverty but not enough to escape poverty altogether.

The situation has only worsened with the recession. In 2011, eight states and the District of Columbia either cut benefits, tightened time limits on how long people can receive benefits, or both.

It is remarkable to me that this country is totally comfortable (as it has always been) denying struggling families in Mississippi the same benefits as those provided in California, while continuing to dole out tax breaks for zillionaires on vacation homes, yachts, and other accoutrements of wealth.

Almost every state now serves a lower percentage of its poor families with children than it did under AFDC and pays a benefit that is worth less than its benefit in the early 1990s, which was in turn lower than it paid in the 1970s. That said, the gap between California on the one hand and Mississippi and Wyoming on the other always was and still is enormous. It is fair to say that—even with its disastrous financial situation—California still offers something that is recognizable as a modest safety net, and Mississippi never did. The even bigger story is what has happened in dozens of other states, including quite a number that have joined Mississippi at the bottom.

With welfare off the table, how do people cope? Kristin Seefeldt of the University of Indiana has interviewed and followed closely a sample of thirty-nine mostly single mothers in Michigan with low incomes, about 60 percent with incomes below the poverty line and a few with incomes as low as $4,000. One key fact, borne out by the statistics mentioned above, is that welfare is on the whole no longer part of the solution.[7]

Most of the women in Seefeldt's sample had always worked when they could find work but, even before the recession, still had substantial periods of unemployment. They received some monetary and in-kind help from extended family and friends, although this became less prevalent with the recession. They did work in the informal economy for people they knew—cooking and child care and hair-braiding, for instance—but again, these possibilities diminished with the recession. One substantial source of help for the small fraction fortunate enough to have it was subsidized housing. Another, more frequent "solution" was moving in with a man who, too often, represented a substantial risk to their physical safety.

Seefeldt found that managing debt was an important (and, again, risky) strategy for the women. They would move frequently to escape accumulated rent and delay paying bills or pay fractions of what was owed to creditors such as utilities that they knew from experience would not breathe down their necks. They would avoid having landline phones in order to be less accessible to bill collectors. Perhaps somewhat surprisingly, many had credit cards that they often used to meet daily living costs and then paid a little here and there on the accumulated debt—just enough, they hoped, to avoid deeper trouble.

Sheila Zedlewski of the Urban Institute and Kathryn Edin, who is now at Harvard, studied ninety-five families that were all living in extreme poverty, without substantial work and without cash assistance.[8] Almost all were mothers living with their children. They mentioned three main reasons for their lack of work. A third were not working because of poor health (and half reported very poor mental or physical health). A quarter could not find a job, and another quarter could not find affordable child care that they trusted. Most were without TANF for one programmatic reason or another—"hassle," sanctions, time limits, or ineligibility. Almost a quarter said they did not want to receive benefits from the government (out of pride or because of the hassle), and about a sixth preferred to get informal child support from their children's fathers without government involvement (and the fact that the government would keep all or most of the support that would be collected).

Like the people in Seefeldt's study, families coped by fragile combinations of erratic child support, sporadic help from family members, periodic help from charities, odd jobs, food stamps, and other in-kind government assistance. Three-quarters received help with housing, whether from the government, extended family, or friends. Not surprisingly, help with housing was key to getting by, however minimally. Only one out of four of the families received all four of food stamps, housing assistance, Medicaid for the adult or adults, and Medicaid for the children. The forthcoming Medicaid coverage for adults in the Affordable Care Act will clearly be very important as an in-kind form of income that will, among other things, enable women to get help for many of the physical and mental problems that keep them out of the job market.

Mathematica Policy Research conducted a similar study of sixteen families in Iowa that had left TANF, had no steady job, and consequently had incomes of less than $500 a month.[9] Not surprisingly, substantial percentages experienced hunger, inability to pay rent, homelessness, and loss of utilities. Like the families in the Urban Institute study, no one was receiving cash assistance. Sources of income were similar to those in the Urban Institute study, with the added insight that people resorted to earning extra money in any way they could, including not only odd jobs but also collecting cans and pawning possessions. Another problem people had was accumulated debt.

To me, the surprise is not in the ways people cope. They do so because it is a human instinct, although to say they are "coping" is somewhat of an overstatement. The bigger surprise is that there are so many people in the United States who are so crushingly poor.

The politics that developed during the Clinton years reflected little understanding of what cash assistance for families with children should be about. Properly understood, it has three purposes: as a temporary safety net; as a bridge to employment (with appropriate support to get from here to there); and, for a small number, as a longer-term support mechanism.

The first purpose is simple: to provide a temporary safety net for people to get back on their feet after some event has thrown them for a loop and left them unexpectedly without enough income to get by. Among other things, it is a gap-filler for an unemployment insurance system that leaves out many people. This is especially important in recessions, but there are people in such situations in the best of times. The five-year time limit in the 1996 law was in theory consistent with this purpose, as was the very name of the new program (although the near-impossibility of getting assistance in many states has now negated even the idea of temporary assistance).

The second purpose—the one that underlay the 1996 law and, in my view, was misconceived nationally and mishandled in most states—related to longer-term recipients who could work but were not doing so. The premise of the 1996 law was that there was an undifferentiated large lump of people, overwhelmingly women, who had chosen to be on the dole and needed nothing more than a swift kick in the behind to get on with their lives in a more productive way.

Why do I say misconceived and mishandled? Because the political consensus was arrived at without an understanding that those who had been on the rolls for a longer period of time were not an undifferentiated group who could all be treated in the same way. It's true that there was a group that, in the hot economy of the late 1990s, was able to find work in response to the stick of the work requirement and the lifetime time limit and the carrot of the EITC, which had been enlarged in 1993; and it's also true that this group included people who should have been prodded toward work much sooner.

But even this group, the most easily employable, did not fare uniformly well. About half of those who found jobs did not escape poverty, and large numbers faced issues such as child care and transportation that got in the way of their holding on to the jobs they got. There were also many who would have done far better if they had been permitted to pursue education and training along with—or as a precursor to—work. But in the first years of the law, three out of five ex-recipients nationally did find work after leaving welfare.

Overall, the share of low-income single mothers with earnings rose from 49 percent in 1995 to 64 percent in 2000. That was good, but it has been dropping ever since, with the number falling to 54 percent by 2009.[10]

Two out of five who left welfare in the early years did so without finding a job.[11] Here is where the second purpose was even more clearly misconceived and mishandled. "Work first"—the mantra of TANF, meaning that going directly to work was to be conclusively preferred to education and training for recipients—was not right for everyone even if they were employable. The track record of pre-employment job-training programs was weak, to be sure, but TANF took a 180-degree turn on this. Many states literally made TANF recipients quit community college or other programs in which they were already enrolled and report instead to unpaid work assignments. Not only should many more have been permitted to pursue education and training, but recipients needed to be assessed on an individual basis and helped with a tailored approach to deal with their particular barriers to success in the workplace. There were mental health issues, especially clinical depression. There were issues of literacy and basic skills associated with a lack of work experience. There were problems of child care, transportation, domestic violence, and substance abuse. These could have been surmounted in many cases, had an individualized plan been developed and implemented.

The messages sent nationally to the states were: number one, get people off the rolls in any way you can; and number two, make everyone go to work (not give everyone the help they need in order to succeed). The new law was a block grant giving the states great flexibility to design their own programs, but the meta-message was two bumper stickers: "Shrink the Rolls" and "Work First for Everyone," supported by strong incentives to induce compliance. Governors coming together at national meetings competed for bragging rights over who had reduced caseloads the most.

There is a third purpose for welfare in a decent society. A relatively small number of people, not legally disabled, are for one reason or another not good candidates for work or are having continued difficulty finding a job. Some of these are the people who now show up in deep poverty because they are unable to get TANF. Many live in rural areas far from jobs. A considerable number have persistent health and mental health problems that are major barriers to success in the workplace but not sufficiently debilitating to make them eligible for disability benefits. Others have chronically ill children or adult relatives who require constant care. These people, who are mostly women, have a strong case for not being required to work outside the home; they may be saving the state millions that would otherwise have to be spent on institutionalization in some form. Still others are continuing victims of domestic violence and require cash assistance if they are to escape. None of these women is legally disabled, but all have a case for not being subject to an arbitrary time limit.

So there is a small residual group that has a good case for not being in the labor market. The 1996 welfare law did throw a bone in their direction by giving the states permission to use federal funds for up to 20 percent of their caseload to continue receiving benefits after the federal five-year time limit expired. In practice, though, most states did not take up the option. The meta-message prevailed—shrink the rolls no matter what.

Welfare has become almost irrelevant in many places as state after state has pursued the overriding goal to pare the rolls and keep them small. They have done so in three ways. One is time limits—not just the five-year limit on federal help, but also shorter time limits that most states adopted in one form or another, as permitted by the federal law. The second is the sanctions policies that throw people off the rolls when they are deemed uncooperative in some way. Twenty-two states gave themselves the power to throw whole families off the rolls the first time they fail to meet a requirement—like missing or showing up late for a meeting with a caseworker because of a car breaking down, a child being ill, or not receiving notice of the meeting at all. Idaho throws people off *for life* after the third infraction.[12] All perfectly legal.

The third and biggest factor, though, is that it is just plain hard to get on TANF. You can't get the rolls down from 14 million to

4 million people without barring the front door. Forty-two states now have formal diversion and job search requirements. Diversion can mean giving people a lump-sum payment to tide them through a temporary emergency in lieu of putting them on the rolls. Applied properly, this can be an excellent way to help people. But too often diversion means that when people apply for welfare, they are told to look for a job—and sometimes must show that they were turned down for perhaps twenty or thirty jobs even when jobs are obviously unavailable—before they will even be considered for TANF. Many employers are so sick of dealing with unsought applicants from the welfare office that they refuse to sign the verification forms the applicants need as proof of the job attempt. Lack of transportation or child care is not accepted as an excuse for not meeting the requirement of making multiple applications. The real point is to discourage people from applying. Many workers at TANF offices simply turn down would-be applicants, telling them that they look employable. Under AFDC, federal law required that every eligible recipient be served. Now there is no legal entitlement to help. The truly shocking fact is that most states have continued to apply their diversion and job-search requirements throughout the current recession. This is why the TANF rolls have risen so modestly during the recession, and have even dropped in many hard-hit states.

The states have also by and large done a poor job of utilizing the best tool they have to keep the rolls in check—namely, helping people get and keep jobs, preferably the best jobs they are capable of holding (provided that jobs are available, of course). In 2005, when the 1996 law was renewed, Congress had before it the fruits of almost a decade of experience and research on what worked and what didn't. One clear finding was that many people with multiple barriers to success can nonetheless succeed, but only if they receive individually tailored services. By 2005, of the fewer than 2 million adults remaining on the rolls, the portion capable of succeeding (other than those in the midst of a temporary stay) was overwhelmingly composed of people needing serious help to do so. Bumper stickers and kicks in the rear weren't going to do it. Yet Congress paid no attention, instead toughening the requirements and sanctions even further, as though the tiny number of longer-term recipients left on the rolls were deadbeats and derelicts.

The unavailability of welfare is a major contributor to deep poverty. In 2002, one out of three people who had left welfare recently had an income below half the poverty level. The percentage of families in deep poverty rose by nearly half between 1994 and 2004, with the unavailability of welfare identified as a major cause of the increase in Arloc Sherman's analysis. A recent Urban Institute study found that one in five low-income single mothers neither worked nor received government cash assistance during the 2004–8 period, as opposed to one in eight in 1996–97.[13]

In light of the current atmosphere in Washington, D.C., TANF is a rare subject where there is broad bipartisan agreement (although, on the Democratic side, not unanimous), but this is a case where bipartisanship is not a good thing. The broad agreement is that TANF is a success—that the welfare rolls have been reduced by 75 percent and that's all anyone needs to know.

A few House members, mainly those in the congressional progressive caucus, and a senator here and there know better. Why so few? Why is the pro-welfare caucus so small they could meet in a phone booth (if one can still be found)?

It goes back to the enactment of the law in 1996. Clinton's support of the bill left Democrats in a quandary. Welfare was a white-hot political issue, an election was imminent, and their president was signaling that he would sign a bill that at least the more progressive among them were inclined to oppose. Yet just twelve senators voted in the fall of 1995 against a version of the bill similar to what was ultimately enacted, and one of those was a right-wing Republican who thought the bill was too liberal. Only one senator up for reelection in 1996, the late Paul Wellstone, voted no. (Twenty-four senators opposed the bill on final passage in 1996.) The lopsided votes in both chambers placed many Democrats in a position where down the road they would have to say it had been a

smashing success, any facts to the contrary notwithstanding. Nonetheless, the facts are to the contrary.

We now know, if we didn't before, that TANF does not do what
a system of cash assistance for families with children should do.
Policy makers rushed to judgment in 1996 and continue to be so
eager to label it a success that they haven't bothered to keep an
eye on it and fix things as problems became evident. Everyone just
prays at the altar of the success of "welfare reform," and most of
them don't have a clue what is happening.

Having said all of that, I want to be clear that there are inherently
difficult problems in finding a solution that works for the largest
number of people. The tough facts—the changes in family structure and the rise of low-wage work in the face of globalization—
mean that even the wisest of policy makers struggle to know exactly
what to do. The difference with the TANF story is that it is a self-
inflicted wound—a place where a politician let a political slogan
get away from him and put millions of lives at risk. There were
some good outcomes in the first few years as well as some very
bad ones, but the situation now is unambiguous. TANF has done
damage from the outset, but its failure to provide a cash safety net
in the face of a recession reveals its true colors with total clarity.

ATTACKING DEEP POVERTY

Every other wealthy industrialized country has a guarantee of a
baseline income, at least for families with children— "family allowances" or "children's allowances" are the usual names for it. These
are generally provided to everyone regardless of their income, and
then recouped from upper-income people through taxes. The payment is modest and is typically the ground floor of a triplex system. The next level is an income-support scheme for those without
work, rather like what our welfare system used to be, except with
national standards that set the level of the payment. Finally, there
is a wage supplement like our EITC.

We have backed into having a baseline of sorts—SNAP—but

at a very low level, barely enough to pay for food. How can we do better? The first step is public awareness, I think. I like to believe that if more people knew how many people have incomes so low that the word "incredible" is not an exaggeration, there would be more of an outcry.

There is a disconnect between our private generosity and our espousal of public policy. *60 Minutes* had a segment about a family with three children that had lost all its income in the recession. They had enough money for one room in an inexpensive motel, but their savings were dwindling fast. All five took to the street with a sign saying they were willing to work doing anything. A local community college hired the father, although even then they did not have enough income to get housing. When the segment aired on *60 Minutes*, contributions poured in and the father got a better job. *60 Minutes* aired the segment a second time as a summer re-run and reported that the family is back on its feet.

There are thousands upon thousands of families who aren't so fortunate. Still, there are additional thousands—although fewer in number—who have also been helped by private charity. But even in this terrible recession—and even with so many people who are brand-new to the ranks of the poor—the willingness to support public policy beyond unemployment compensation is limited (and even unemployment compensation is still not available to very low-wage and part-time workers). And the willingness to support continuance of extended unemployment benefits to those who do qualify is wearing thin.

Perhaps the best argument for a more satisfactory baseline income is new research in brain development and family dynamics that evidences a clear tie between childhood poverty—especially poverty in early childhood—and deleterious outcomes down the road. Research cited by the preeminent researcher Greg Duncan and his colleague Katherine Magnuson shows higher educational performance and better employment outcomes when low-income families receive even modest increases in income. They cite re-search that a sustained $3,000 increase in the income of families with young children who have incomes below $25,000 is associated with a 17 percent increase in adult earnings. In the early years of a child's schooling, such an income increase is associated with an advance in achievement of 20 percent of a school year.[14]

I have lifted up the question of deep poverty for special attention because of its serious magnitude and the fact that it is largely ignored by the media and politicians. But the remedy for deep poverty cannot function in isolation. As I said earlier, food stamps are not merely an income stream for those with no other income. Their function is to serve as much or even more as an income supplement for people who have low-wage work. A cash component of a baseline income, a proper version of TANF, should also serve—by all reason, with nationally determined benefit levels—as both a baseline income and an income supplement. At the same time—and this is very important—TANF should be a takeoff point to a job or some other road to self-sufficiency for most of the people who receive it.

If we are ever to get past the stigmatization of TANF recipients, we need to stop looking at them as though they are a separate category of people. The vast majority of them go in and out of jobs. They want to get work and provide for their children like all other parents. We need to design a meaningful job-oriented system to help them do what they want to do, including education and training as appropriate. Our pejorative view of TANF recipients and the ensuing shrinkage of TANF to near-extinction have contributed to a phenomenal expansion of extreme poverty in this wealthy nation.

6

Concentrated Poverty: "The Abandoned"

In his book *Disintegration: The Splintering of Black America*, the Pulitzer Prize–winning *Washington Post* columnist Eugene Robinson uses the phrase "The Abandoned."[1] Our nation can justly celebrate the progress of African American achievement since World War II, but there is a distinct, and awful, exception: the opening of a yawning gap between those who have made it and those who have not. Racism and racial discrimination have hardly disappeared, but for some millions of African Americans, the problem is one of class as well as race.

The abandoned in Robinson's rendering are the people many Americans think of first when they think about poverty—the African American poor who live in the inner city. But the abandoned of our nation are not only African American, and they are not only residents of inner cities. They are Native Americans on reservations; former coal miners in Appalachia; seasonal farmworkers in California, Florida, and elsewhere; sharecroppers in Alabama and Mississippi; and day laborers in city after city.

My concern in this chapter is primarily the abandoned who live in the inner city, disproportionately but far from exclusively African American: people who live amid conditions of concentrated, persistent, and intergenerational poverty far more than the rest of the poor. Robinson's examples are the Lower Ninth Ward in New Orleans—which temporarily came into broader public view because of Hurricane Katrina—and neighborhoods east of the Anacostia River in the District of Columbia.

The inner-city poor are a fairly small minority of the poor overall, but they are the central players in the political drama about poverty, especially those who are African American. These are the quintessential places where race, poverty, and politics intersect, with awful results. They are places of continual human tragedy: violent streets, distressingly few youth graduating from high school, prisons and jails filled with young men from the area, too many teenagers having babies and large numbers of women raising children by themselves, rampant drug and alcohol abuse, children abused physically and sexually, staggering AIDS rates—the list goes on.

There are success stories, to be sure: young people who do squeeze through the inverted funnel that allows a few to make it out. The neighborhoods are far from monolithic. If 40 percent of residents are poor, 60 percent are not, and many of the poor are working, too. There are stalwart residents who stay in the community and provide leadership and a measure of stability. But the contrasts between high-poverty and low-poverty neighborhoods are stark on every dimension, whether it is the number of people not completing high school, the number married or never married, the number unemployed, or any of many other parameters. Somehow, though, we do not see the linkages that tie everything together and cry out for an all-points response. In its totality it is catastrophic.

What I see as catastrophic others label a massive failure of personal responsibility. Who can disagree with the proposition that people have to behave responsibly? That isn't the question. The question is what we can do to help people take responsibility for themselves and their children on a more consistent basis. Children being born in the inner city today are not born into the Garden of Eden. The original sin occurred long ago. They are growing up in a toxic environment that poses formidable odds against their success or even their sheer survival. Unraveling the tangle of problems will not occur because someone snaps his fingers and says the people of the inner city have to act responsibly.

This is tough stuff. Whether we are talking about the inner city, Appalachia, or Indian reservations, we are talking about too many poor people all living in the same place and for a long time—long enough for behaviors to be passed on from one generation to the next and reinforced among peers in each generation as it comes along.

One has only to look at the foster care rolls in Washington, D.C., to see how hard it is. Seventy-six percent of the intake of D.C.'s child welfare protection agency in 2009 were children born to teen parents or to women who had their first child as a teen. "Why do the mothers not know what they are doing to their own life prospects and the prospects of the children to whom they give birth?" I asked a brilliant young lawyer I know who represents these girls.

She said, "They think they're not good at anything but believe that they will be good mothers."

"But don't they know the trouble they're headed for?" I asked.

She said, "Their mothers had them out of wedlock and in some cases their grandmothers had their mothers out of wedlock, and many of their friends are also having children out of wedlock." This is tough stuff.

It doesn't help to talk about a "culture of poverty." But it also doesn't help to gloss over the statistics and the behaviors they represent. The behaviors have to be addressed not with more punitive and pejorative approaches—we've had enough of those—but with answers that combine structural reform with one-on-one approaches that encourage and support personal responsibility.

A host of changes needs to happen in order to create better support for positive behaviors. Getting good behaviors is difficult without fairly consistent incentives. Some of what we need to do is structural. Better schools, real opportunities for college and careers, more people working, increased incomes, a fairer criminal justice system, safer streets, good health care, and decent social services are all important. But the structural changes aren't enough. The behaviors have to be addressed.

Are there things we can do to promote personal and parental

responsibility? Absolutely. Positive role models are vital, especially for young people. Parents, especially young parents, can learn how to be better parents through classes at their children's child care centers and schools. Home visiting can be valuable if it is done competently and on a wholly voluntary basis. The Parent-Child Home Program, which serves seven thousand families annually in 150 communities in fourteen states, is a good example. HIPPY, which I discuss later in this chapter, is another. Schools can teach nonviolence and the importance of civic participation. Churches can play a more active role by mobilizing parishioners to be tutors and mentors. Community and neighborhood leaders of all kinds have an obligation to play a constructive role.

This is an area where I think liberals and conservatives have been talking past each other. To call for personal responsibility is not to "blame the victim." No one succeeds in life without taking personal responsibility, but the tools of opportunity need to exist as well. And we need to broaden the conversation.

The issues here are ones of both race and class. Insofar as we are talking about the African American community, we should be clear: while the whole society has an obligation to do far more, the African American community has a special obligation to confront the issues of class in its own ranks. Too much of the abandoning is being done by other African Americans—some of it proactively and some by dereliction of civic duty. Make no mistake: there are African American heroes working hard and making a difference in every neighborhood and in every walk of life. There are heroes who are teaching and mentoring children, building houses, helping ex-offenders to break through the monumental barriers they face, and on and on. But there are bad facts, too. Too many of the teachers who are failing poor African American children are themselves African American. Too many police who are arresting and prison guards who are guarding African American young people with what I would politely call excessive zeal are themselves African American. Too many of the workers at the welfare office who are turning African American applicants away when they could do otherwise are themselves African American. In general, too many African Americans who are doing better see the poor people in their own community as the "other."

So the central issue explored in this chapter is the issue of place—too many poor people living in one locality. It is not an issue unique to one race or ethnicity, and it exists in rural areas as well as cities, but in this chapter I focus mainly on the inner city. Poverty produces a lot of bad outcomes, but they are not nearly as terrible either qualitatively or quantitatively as they are when the poverty is concentrated. The poverty in inner cities, in Appalachia, in the Black Belt of the South, and on Indian reservations is more persistent and more intergenerational and therefore even harder to tackle than poverty generally.

An up-to-the-minute picture of inner-city concentrated poverty is hard to draw, but the situation is clearly worse than it was a decade ago. After 2000, the census made major changes in its methodology and no longer collects decennial information about income, race, and ethnicity broken down by census tract, apparently for budgetary reasons. The more recent information comes from the American Community Survey (ACS), which presents a rolling average from 2005–9. It is based on small sample sizes that experts find less reliable, but it tells us pretty clearly that, like poverty generally and deep poverty in particular, concentrated poverty has worsened since 2000.

The 2000 picture was quite striking, in a good way. Urban Institute expert Thomas Kingsley called it "astonishing." The number of poor people living in high-poverty neighborhoods dropped significantly compared to 1990. The proportion that was African American also went down. The only areas in the country that saw notable increases were in California and the Southwest, and to a more modest extent in the Northeast. The reason for the overall improvement, quite obviously, was the hot economy of the late 1990s.[2]

Census tracts (neighborhoods and areas of about four thousand people) with poverty at 40 percent or above are what is generally thought of as concentrated poverty. Concentrated poverty rose steadily from 1970 through 1990 and then dropped in the 1990s. The share of the metropolitan poor living in places of concentrated poverty went from 13 to 17 percent between 1980 and 1990, and then dropped back to 12 percent in 2000. Those in large urban areas were about 46 percent black, 37 percent Hispanic, and 11 percent non-Hispanic white.[3]

A recent Brookings Institution analysis concluded that the number of poor people living in concentrated poverty in metropolitan areas went up by 34.5 percent from 2000 to the years 2005–9, and was probably much higher by 2010.[4] It nearly doubled in the Midwest and rose by a third in the South, while the Northeast and the West were generally unchanged. The number of high-poverty census tracts went up by 54 percent in the suburbs, compared to an increase of 18 percent in the cities. The Brookings analysis suggests that overall we are nearly back to 1990 levels, although there has been a substantial change in the location of the problem.

Washington, D.C., has one of the highest proportions of census tracts with concentrated poverty. The poverty level in Ward 8, the poorest in the city, went from 27 percent in both 1980 and 1990 to 36 percent in 2000 (which ought to be a fact of far greater concern locally than has been the actual case), to 35 percent for 2005–9. The deterioration during the 1990s is especially of concern, since that was a "good" decade for poverty nationally.

A look at states with high percentages of concentrated poverty reveals the racial and ethnic mix involved: southern states with African Americans, West Virginia with whites, South Dakota with Native Americans, Arizona and New Mexico with Latinos and Native Americans, California and New York with African Americans and Latinos.[5]

High-poverty neighborhoods in the West and Southwest look different from those typical of the rest of the country. For example, City Heights in San Diego—the site of a major neighborhood revitalization initiative originally spearheaded by the late Sol Price (founder of Price Clubs)—is 57 percent Latino, 18 percent Asian,

13 percent black (including the second-largest Somali population in the United States), 8 percent white, and 4 percent other.[6] City Heights is distinctive in another way, one that is often the case with high-poverty neighborhoods that aren't African American: it is heavily immigrant, and that means it has a high turnover. People move out as quickly as they can. It's still a place of concentrated poverty, but many of the poor who live there are not the same people from one year or decade to the next.

The fundamental strategic question of this chapter is what we need to do to deconcentrate the poverty of the inner cities. Should we ideally be trying to get everyone out of the inner city, dispersed into racially and economically integrated neighborhoods throughout metropolitan areas? Or should we try to raise up the inner city so that it works as a healthy community with the vast majority of its residents steadily employed? Or, as I believe is the case, is there a "mixed" strategy that pursues both goals and gives people a genuine choice about where they will live?

If the problems are not new, neither are the efforts to solve them.

ROBERT KENNEDY
AND BEDFORD-STUYVESANT

The inner city was at the forefront of concerns about race in the 1960s. As Dr. King and so many others worked courageously and nonviolently to end apartheid in the South, violence fueled by impatience over joblessness and discrimination was appearing elsewhere, finally exploding in Watts in the summer of 1965. It was almost certainly not coincidental that the Watts rebellion began eleven days after President Johnson signed the historic Voting Rights Act. The new law meant less than nothing to young people in inner cities who felt hemmed in, physically and otherwise, with no prospect for escape.

In November 1965, Senator Kennedy asked me and my colleague Adam Walinsky to work on ideas for addressing poverty in the inner cities. He had spoken out strongly after the riots, but now he wanted to follow up with specific proposals. He had denounced the violence, but he also believed that urban poverty raised profound questions of economic justice—in his view, the major civil rights challenge facing the nation after the fight to dismantle American apartheid.

The segregation of American cities had a long history. Going north and west in the Great Migration beginning roughly at the end of World War I, African Americans had for decades found themselves directed to particular neighborhoods whether they wanted to be there or not. Public policy and private discrimination worked in tandem to bring this about. Overt federal policy as well as banking predilections made it impossible for African Americans to buy or rent housing outside of the segregated areas. They could not get mortgages even in the segregated neighborhoods, except from the tiny African American–owned banks that existed here and there. With few exceptions, the only African Americans able to purchase homes were those who could pay cash (with consequences for asset-building that last to this day). Public housing location decisions also reinforced the segregation.

Until the late 1960s, the segregated neighborhoods, poor as they were, were communities where business owners, doctors, lawyers, teachers, preachers, and morticians all lived side by side along with everyone else. Unemployment was higher than in the white community, but some factory jobs and other manual labor were available, although the economic framework had begun to fray after World War II with the return of veterans reclaiming their position in the labor market. And some neighborhoods were destroyed by the urban renewal policies of the 1950s ("Negro removal," as it was termed in the African American community). Nonetheless, until the 1960s, there was (at least as people who grew up there think of it now) a sense of community and stability, segregated as it was.

Things started to deteriorate economically in the 1960s. Even as the civil rights movement was dismantling American apartheid, the economics of the inner city began to get worse. The economic changes in the bigger world outside hit the inner city the hardest.

Unemployment was rampant, especially among young people. Their anger boiled over in Watts and in inner cities across the country.

Adam and I came up with ideas for three speeches, to be delivered by Kennedy at three venues where he was scheduled to speak in January 1966. They had two major themes: how to bring about racial and economic desegregation throughout metropolitan areas and how to revitalize neighborhoods of concentrated poverty in inner cities.

Racial and economic desegregation were vitally important but also difficult to achieve. As for neighborhood revitalization, Kennedy laid out an idea that Adam had recommended. Outside funding and investment, both public and private, would support economic development and the upgrading of housing and community facilities. The visionary part of the idea was that jobs could be created for local people to work on improving their own housing and their own communities. At the start of the first speech in the trilogy, Kennedy said his reason for speaking was "to suggest that our purpose to help the Northern Negro must pervade every plan we make for the future of our cities."[7]

Perhaps sooner than he anticipated, Kennedy saw an opportunity to put the neighborhood revitalization idea into practice. One evening, a month or so after delivering the three speeches, he met with leaders of the predominantly African American neighborhood of Bedford-Stuyvesant in Brooklyn. Their mood was one of urgency. Watts was much on their mind and they were worried about what would happen if nothing was done to reduce the high levels of joblessness and poverty in their own backyard. They challenged Kennedy to help them.

Kennedy outlined his plan and—after getting a positive reaction from his audience and others with whom he subsequently spoke— decided to proceed. In the following months he flew to New York two or even three times a week to work on bringing the project to life. There was extensive community wrangling as people pushed to get a piece of the action, and there were protracted negotiations with Mayor John Lindsay, Governor Nelson Rockefeller, and key business and financial leaders over what they and other outside actors would do to help.

When the dust finally settled, the result was the Bedford-Stuyvesant Restoration Corporation. Led by Franklin Thomas, who later headed the Ford Foundation, it did not feature Adam Walinsky's idealistic image of sweat equity rebuilding the neighborhood, but it nonetheless contained a most ambitious idea: an inside-outside partnership that would revitalize a deeply troubled place, combining, as Robert Kennedy said at its dedication, "the best of community action with the best of the private-enterprise system." Its work, still going on today, was to build and renovate housing, finance home ownership, promote economic development, and sponsor arts and cultural activities.

Equally important, Kennedy and his senior colleague from the state, Republican Senator Jacob Javits, succeeded in amending the Economic Opportunity Act—the war on poverty legislation—to authorize federal funding for initiatives like the Bedford-Stuyvesant Restoration Corporation. These funds, distinctive in that proposals for their use could be tailored to the particular needs of a revitalizing neighborhood, seeded dozens of similar endeavors around the country during the decade or so that they were available.

With the addition of significant funding from the Ford Foundation and other sources, the result today is more than two thousand community development corporations (CDCs), as well as numerous other inner-city development organizations and outside entities that help finance their activities. Organizations such as the Local Initiatives Support Corporation, Enterprise Community Partners, NeighborWorks America, and their many individual local counterparts have made a tangible and important difference in building and rehabilitating housing for low-income people and promoting economic development in low-income neighborhoods.

Was Bedford-Stuyvesant a success? Yes and no. Yes, for sure, in the sense of tangible results in the neighborhood: 2,200 units of housing built or renovated, mortgage financing for nearly 1,500 homeowners, $475 million in investments in the neighborhood, 20,000 people placed in jobs, the Billie Holiday Theatre, and so on. But no in the sense that the sum of all this isn't nearly enough. To the extent that we thought in the heady spirit of the time that one super-duper community development corporation could do it all, we were overly optimistic. The work of a CDC has to be a cog in a larger social-policy apparatus to revitalize an inner-city neighborhood and needs to have an economic strategy that gets people to jobs outside the neighborhood. And, not long after Kennedy's death, the nation began a long turning away from the kinds of promising social policy initiatives he championed. He would be shocked to see how little meaningful attention we have paid—and continue to pay—to the inner city.

FROM KENNEDY TO CLINTON

We have learned a lot since the Bedford-Stuyvesant CDC was created, but the vexing question of concentrated urban poverty is still with us. In the meantime, though, the realities of the inner city have worsened. Since Kennedy's time, we have seen massive changes in the job market, the flight of higher-income people from the inner city, the conservative drift in our politics, the increase in births to unmarried mothers, crack cocaine, and the AIDS epidemic. Some of these facts are the behavioral consequences of concentrated poverty. Others reflect failures of strategy and policy in both the design and implementation of efforts that have been undertaken.

There were also issues within the CDC movement itself, which encompassed some strange bedfellows with very different motives. Some of the neighborhood people who joined to form CDCs had a political agenda of black power and community control. They were happy to accept outside resources and get outside employers to locate plants and stores in their neighborhoods, but their underlying purpose was to use those things as a means to create a self-contained economy and power base within the four corners of their immediate environs. That economy would contain its own engines, and—living together in a same-race community—the community development corporations would become a cohesive and effective force in municipal politics.

On the other hand, some of those who assisted from the outside were only too happy to do so as a strategy to mute possible demands for metropolitan desegregation. Consciously or unconsciously, some of the mayors and civic leaders and foundation heads could see a value in getting inner-city residents to stay where they were.

A centerpiece of the Bed-Stuy strategy was an IBM manufacturing plant located there by RFK's friend Tom Watson, the company's CEO. The ease with which IBM's cooperation was obtained led to an assumption that others of similar magnitude would follow. They did not. Yet the notion that an economic revival could be accomplished within the borders of the neighborhood continued to hold sway.

Few revitalization initiatives responded to the reality that, in most cities, the jobs were increasingly located in the suburbs, largely inaccessible to inner-city residents in the absence of specific initiatives to get them there. Nor were the antidiscrimination laws enforced as rigorously as they should have been. These shortfalls, coupled with negative attitudes of some inner-city residents—especially men—toward white employers, diminished employment outcomes only a bus or subway ride away.

Equally troubling, few neighborhood revitalization initiatives sought to play a role in improving the education that neighborhood children were receiving. Would-be workers needed to be better educated and trained, and the local schools were falling down on the job, to say the least. One exception was the Sandtown-Winchester neighborhood effort in Baltimore—started by the late James Rouse, who had given the world Columbia, Maryland; the Baltimore Harbor; and the Faneuil Hall Marketplace in Boston—which took on responsibility for its local elementary schools in the mid-1990s.

My point here is not that Bedford-Stuyvesant was a perfect model or that CDCs and similar organizations in general were a perfect model. As applied, they tended to have the flaws I have noted, and at their best they do not represent an all-encompassing strategy. But they have a role to play. They have made important contributions especially in the areas of housing and economic development and will properly be a part of ongoing efforts. What those efforts should look like is the subject of the rest of this chapter.

The triple whammy of a national economy unwelcoming of people with incomes below the national median, the consequent intensification of inner-city poverty, and the weak public policy responses to both problems meant that neighborhood-revitalization efforts also operated against great odds after 1968. The general waning of interest in problems of the inner city once the civil unrest of the 1960s had been contained added to the difficulty of getting things done.

Not that the inner city was off the table completely. As we have noted, its residents became the stuff of racial politics—both Reagan's "welfare queen" and the first Bush's Willie Horton.

Why the Democrats had no effective response is not easy to answer. One way to answer is to ask what would have happened if Robert Kennedy had lived since he was so especially interested in the inner city (regardless of whether he would have been elected president). Kennedy (and, in a more traditionally liberal way, Hubert Humphrey) represented the urban and minority base of the Democratic Party, although RFK appealed to other constituencies as well. George McGovern, despite his wonderful work on hunger, was more attuned to a suburban, environmental, dovish, and highly process-oriented constituency. Beginning with Kennedy's death and Humphrey's decline, the party turned away from its urban roots. Maybe this was just an artifact of demographics, with the balance of power relocating to the suburbs and the Sunbelt, but perhaps different national leadership in the party would have paid positive attention to the problems in the inner city and not left those issues to be exploited by the political operatives of the right. And maybe Robert Kennedy was one of a kind.

ENTERPRISE ZONES
AND EMPOWERMENT ZONES

There was constant neighborhood-revitalization activity all over the country all through the 1970s and 1980s. There was the Watts Labor Community Action Committee in Los Angeles, the New Community Corporation in Newark, the Woodlawn Organization and later the Steans Foundation in Chicago, the work of James Rouse in Baltimore and of Price Charities in San Diego, and many others in many cities. They were making a difference then and they still are today.

In the late 1980s, Jack Kemp reintroduced the issue to national policy. The former quarterback, conservative to the core in believing tax cuts would solve every American problem, had a distinctly iconoclastic view among Republicans about the politics of race and about race itself. Invoking the memory of Robert Kennedy and Bedford-Stuyvesant, as well as experience in Great Britain under the Conservative government of Margaret Thatcher, Kemp applied his tax-cutting faith to the inner city and proposed a scheme called enterprise zones, a British term. Kennedy—as we know, not a traditional liberal—had indeed introduced legislation to offer tax incentives to stimulate plant location in inner cities (and a companion bill that targeted rural areas). Kemp's idea was in the same vein, except that Kennedy's idea was part of a comprehensive strategy, quite different from a pure supply-side approach. Thinking that tax incentives would do the job in and of themselves was not a sound idea, but at least it was an idea. Quite a few localities and a few states tried using tax incentives to stimulate housing and economic development in blighted neighborhoods but, usually lacking a three-dimensional approach, did not accomplish much.

Bill Clinton's election produced another chapter in the story—Empowerment Zones. Recruited to the president's economic team was a Michigan lawyer and law professor named Paul Dimond who had a career-long interest in inner-city revitalization. Dimond, who was nothing if not single-minded, thought enterprise zones (in the sense of tax incentives) could work if they were coupled with direct federal funding and a requirement for a collaborative local planning process. Dimond talked to everybody whose ear he could bend, and the result was that the White House sent his idea to Capitol Hill.

Senator Bill Bradley and Congressman Charles Rangel picked up the idea, and it was enacted in May 1993. What happened was a modest example of why people say passing bills is like making sausage. Then, as now, there wasn't a lot of money available, but there were a lot of members of Congress who wanted a piece of the action. What was created sounded big—a billion-dollar investment that would make funding available to 104 urban and rural communities, over and above the value of the various tax incentives created by the legislation. The smaller print clarified that the billion was over a ten-year period, although—unlike many other programs—the appropriation would be made all at once so that it wouldn't be subject to the annual vicissitudes of the congressional budgeting process. And while there were indeed to be 104 recipient communities, only nine amounted to anything. The nine (six urban and three rural) would be called empowerment zones (EZs). The urban zones would receive $100 million each, and the rural zones would each get $30 million. Each of the ninety-five other communities, called enterprise communities (ECs), would receive just under $2.9 million. Even the bigger urban-zone money was actually a pittance, apart from the tax incentives—$10 million a year when you broke it down—and the law required that it be divided among three neighborhoods in each city.[8]

We might have thought we had learned from history. The Model Cities program in the 1960s, a federal initiative to use holistic approaches against poverty in low-income neighborhoods, had also suffered from having its funding spread too thin. By the time Congress had finished with Model Cities, it had diluted the money so as to spread it to nearly two hundred communities. Then, during the Nixon years, the ever-present appetite of state and local officials for federal money without strings and performance measures carried the day, and Model Cities became Community Development Block Grants (CDBGs). Clearly, some of the CDBG funds over the years have helped low-income neighborhoods, but it is impossible to know how much because cities are permitted to use the funds in so many different ways, and tracking is inadequate to say the least. On the other hand, if Model Cities had been targeted to the thirty highest-priority cities, it might have lacked the political support to be enacted in the first place.

Bradley and Rangel did one other thing. They structured the legislation to make it a part of Title XX of the Social Security Act, which brought me into it. Why? Because, as part of Title XX, the money would be appropriated to the Department of Health and Human Services (HHS), where I was working, instead of directly to the Department of Housing and Urban Development and the Department of Agriculture, which were tasked with giving out the money. Bradley and Rangel used Title XX because it was under their jurisdiction as members of the Senate Finance and House Ways and Means Committees.

Donna Shalala, my boss at HHS, is an urbanist by training. She told the White House that she could not be statutorily responsible for the funds without having a say in how they would be spent and put me in charge of HHS's participation. A five-way steering committee was created, with representatives of the White House, the vice president's office (Vice President Al Gore had been tapped by President Clinton to oversee the program), and the three departments.

Understanding that the statute wasn't written the way we would have written it and that the funding was less than it should have been, we dove in. We wrote a request for proposals that we thought was quite good, requiring a collaborative and participatory planning process that created local structures that had a lasting salutary effect in some areas—even in some places that didn't get funded. We required a showing of what state and local funds would be put into the implementation, and in some cities the response was impressive—$200 million in New York, for example ($100 million from the state and $100 million from the city).

The program had some good outcomes, particularly in New York City and Philadelphia. My niece, Deborah Wright, was in charge of the Harlem portion of the effort in New York and produced some quite tangible outcomes in housing and economic development. I asked Debbie what the three top accomplishments of the New York EZ were during her four years at the helm, from 1996 to 1999. She listed developing a comprehensive business plan to create jobs by investing in industries already thriving in New York City but not in Harlem (tourism, business services, and education); catalytic investment in Harlem USA, the first meaningful retail development in decades, anchored by a Magic Johnson Theatre; and creation of a $25 million investment pool specifically targeting cultural institutions.

Debbie thinks the work was at a significant enough scale that there was some synergism in its neighborhood effects, particularly because of the added infusion of money from the state and the city. There was certainly quite a bit of gentrification in Harlem bringing some of the change but, especially because there is so much public housing there, the neighborhood still has a large number of low-income people. The commercial investments were helped by the middle-income influx, but the lower-income people definitely benefited as well. The Pathmark supermarket that opened brought nationally competitive prices to the area, as did other new ventures, and the Pathmark store became the most profitable in the whole chain. The stores in Harlem USA, as well as Pathmark and others that came along, hired a substantial number of young workers who would be out of luck in other inner cities. The quality of community life improved across the board. These kinds of interactive results are exactly what we want to see from neighborhood revitalization initiatives. Obviously the Empowerment Zone didn't make good things happen all by itself, but it helped significantly.

Philadelphia mayor (later Pennsylvania governor) Ed Rendell pursued a combined economic development and social services strategy in three Philadelphia neighborhoods. The EZ made 223 loans to 139 businesses, attracted 460 new businesses, leveraged more than $100 million in private investment, and created two-thousand-plus jobs for EZ residents. The urban landscape initiative built five community service facilities, including the Althea Gibson Community Education and Tennis Center, and hauled away twenty-two tons of trash. The EZ's twelve housing initiatives rehabilitated 304 homes.

On the other hand, Bill Campbell, the mayor of Atlanta who later went to jail for tax evasion, squandered the money without any visible outcome, and Chicago mayor Richard Daley distributed the funds in a highly politicized way for which there was little to show at the end of the day.

Perhaps the empowerment zone program would have matured into an interesting effort if it had been permitted to develop further; what happened in Harlem is one indication. But the Gingrich revolution wasn't supportive of the empowerment zones. There was a second, more modest round of funding in 1998 that added some additional empowerment zone designations and a third in 2001 that awarded only eligibility for tax incentives. The last round of tax incentives was meant to expire in 2009 but was extended until the end of 2011 as an antirecessionary measure. President Clinton was able to get other economic development tax incentives enacted late in his second term, but, not surprisingly, the George W. Bush era saw little new activity in this area.

WHAT DOES THE FUTURE LOOK LIKE?

What would make a difference? A hot economy would. In every respect, a strong economy is our strongest antipoverty weapon, even when it helps the rich more than the poor. When there's a hot economy, there are more jobs and all of the jobs pay a little better. We had a hot economy in the second half of the 1990s. It did have a positive impact on life in the inner cities. Unemployment went down and income from work went up. The big increase in the Earned Income Tax Credit that had been added by legislation in 1986, 1990, and 1993 bumped up the incentive for single mothers to work and added income to those who already had a low-wage job.

A neighborhood that has more people working is going to be a healthier neighborhood. We saw some evidence of that in the late 1990s. There will still be problems—lousy schools, environmental justice issues like lead poisoning and toxic dumps, and crime rates higher than those in the rest of the city. But two things that the brief economic sunshine of the late 1990s told us are (1) if there is a better income mix, there will be a better neighborhood; and (2) trends concerning poverty aren't always bad and getting worse, even on seemingly intractable fronts. Poverty rates plunged in the late 1990s, and people who had been denigrated and stereotyped proved that they were quite willing and able to work. Things can improve.

There are two ways to achieve a better income mix in a neighborhood. One is more work and better pay for the people already there. The other is to get people with higher incomes to move in. This one is only applicable in generally healthy cities with a central core identity and, in any event, it has risks. Who is moving in? Are they people who want to be part of the community that was already there? That's good. Or are they people who would prefer that those already there disappear? In other words, gentrification gone bad. The hot economy had a downside that continued through the housing bubble: gentrification that in too many instances pushed poor people out.

Nonetheless, there is some new thinking about remedies for concentrated urban poverty and, despite the challenges posed by gentrification, the new thinking has begun to affect public policy and civic action. Fueled by federal funding to deconcentrate public housing, a new generation of developers has produced mixed-income housing in some low-income neighborhoods. The Harlem Children's Zone and other school ventures have offered new educational initiatives that combine excellent schools with services addressing the problems associated with the ubiquitous poverty of the children they serve. Finally, there are some new schemes to help inner-city residents get and keep jobs in the regional economy.

At the same time, it is important to acknowledge the significant impact—largely negative for the poor, I would argue—that gentrification has had. Bad or good, in some cities it is the biggest change in residential patterns since suburbanization and exurbanization. With major exceptions such as Detroit and Phoenix (for quite different reasons), people have rediscovered the central city as an attractive place to live. Young singles and couples, especially before their children are of school age, and baby boomers with empty nests have voted with their feet (at least until the recession set in) to settle in or return to central-city locations.

This is desirable in many ways. Mayors love the increase in their tax bases and residents who don't have a disproportionate need for municipal services. A vibrant central city is great for business, especially the entertainment business. A sense of life and energy is great all around. But things get more complicated when the neighborhoods moved to are predominantly poor, which has happened in many cities. Radical change has occurred almost overnight in low-income neighborhoods that are easily accessible to downtown, have a sound housing stock, and are adjacent to higher-income areas. Too often, the existing residents find themselves pushed out by skyrocketing rents and property taxes.

Some older residents have chosen, quite happily (before housing prices plummeted), to sell their homes and go back to the South. Too many others, though, have dispersed in directions unknown and all too often to circumstances less desirable than where they previously were. To the extent that those pushed out (and new immigrants as well) end up in inner-ring suburbs, new challenges posed by concentrated poverty show up in places even less equipped to respond with transit and other necessary services and community-development strategies. Some cities have adopted circuit-breakers that slow the pace of property tax increases on lower-income homeowners to help them stay where they are, but in general it is difficult to stem the tide of the market, wholly apart from whether there is any political will to do so.

Overall, gentrification is not an unalloyed good or bad, but rather an urban reality that policy makers have a responsibility to manage in order to minimize displacement and preserve social fabrics. In some cities, it has changed the playing field regarding concentrated poverty, at least in neighborhoods that are attractive to higher-income people.

What is the strategic point here? My view has always been that our society functions best when no one is consigned by law or a multiplicity of facts and forces to live in a certain part of a city. The ideas in this chapter are premised on the idea of real choice. This means policies that directly promote deconcentration in a metropolitan framework and policies to strengthen inner-city neighborhoods both to empower people to move if they want to and to build a stronger community for those who prefer to stay where they are.

Housing: The HOPE VI Experience

If gentrification is one trend changing the face of concentrated poverty, another is the demolition of inner-city public housing and the accompanying dispersal of its residents. This has occurred under HOPE VI, the Homeownership and Opportunities for People Everywhere Act, enacted in 1992. The original idea behind HOPE VI was to weed out unsatisfactory public housing and replace it with mixed-income developments without reducing the supply of housing for low-income people. But the fact is that HOPE VI has significantly dented the national inventory of public housing and forcibly relocated tenants in large numbers (although it hasn't had much effect on the overall level of inner-city poverty in most localities).[9]

The numbers are quite large, and the effect on the public-housing inventory is significant. HUD has made about 250 HOPE VI public-housing revitalization grants, which eventuated in the demolition of almost a hundred thousand public housing units and the relocation of seventy-thousand-plus households. Around 111,000 new and rehabilitated units were developed, including 53,000 units of public housing. In all, the total public-housing stock has decreased by about 12 percent from the 1.33 million units available in 1995.[10] That's a lot. Yet it's important to remember that the number of families who were relocated is only a tiny fraction of the inner-city poor.

So how should we think about HOPE VI? Opinions are divided, even among liberals.

On the one hand, Bruce Katz, a former senior HUD official and highly respected housing and urban policy expert, says, "HOPE VI is one of the most successful urban redevelopment initiatives of the past half-century."[11] On the other hand, Sheila Crowley, the president and CEO of the National Low-Income Housing Coalition, calls it "a case study in how badly a national program can run amok."[12]

Crowley and others point out that the country lost 12 percent of its public-housing inventory at a time when the supply of affordable housing was steadily shrinking and urban rents were going through the roof. Many low-income people were moved whether they wanted to be or not. And the demolished housing was replaced by mixed-income developments with far fewer units for low-income people than the projects they replaced. In some instances, HOPE VI amounted to a federally subsidized land grab for developers and gentrifiers.

By contrast, HOPE VI's adherents stress the awfulness of the projects that were demolished, Cabrini-Green in Chicago being a prime example. They also cite examples of mixed-income developments that are not only successful, but in some cases have brought about decreases in the poverty rate in their surrounding neighborhoods. Chicago public-interest lawyer Alexander Polikoff lists examples from Atlanta, Baltimore, Charlotte, Milwaukee, Cleveland, and San Francisco where neighborhoods in which a HOPE VI development was situated experienced subsequent decreases in poverty of 10 percent or more.

The core of the difference between the contending sides is a fierce argument between those who see HOPE VI as destroying communities—however troubled they may be—and reducing the inventory of badly needed public housing and those who see it as helping people escape the ravages of concentrated poverty. The critics of HOPE VI see the involuntary relocation of people as no different from the much-maligned urban-renewal policies of half a century ago. Supporters see the relocation efforts as pathways to a better life and avenues toward racial and economic desegregation as well. They stress that most of the previous residents do not want to return to the neighborhood and are glad to have the housing vouchers that enable them (although not always without difficulty) to move to a neighborhood they find more desirable.

Who is right? Much of the public housing that was torn down was inherently unlivable or had become so. But, at least in hindsight, it does appear that a larger investment in support services would have helped people find more suitable housing and adjust more satisfactorily to their new surroundings. My heart is with deconcentration. We know there are problems both ways. At the very least, deconcentrating at scale is a tall order. But I believe we have a better chance of breaking the cycle of concentration effects relatively more quickly with dispersion strategies. Especially with inner-city neighborhoods that are not close to downtown areas, I think the possibility of attracting in-migration is slim. And while I put somewhat more hope in improving educational and employment outcomes for current inner-city residents, I think breaking through the consequences of concentration is very hard.

But we should not make hasty judgments. It may take a generation or more to see the real outcomes of HOPE VI. I still think that, done right, it is the preferable road to take, although neighborhood-based strategies must go on as well.

Education as an Organizing Principle

Going back to Robert Kennedy, the "gold standard" for dealing with high-poverty neighborhoods has for decades been the idea of tackling the problems holistically. The insight of Bedford-Stuyvesant and others of the time was that the issues couldn't be confronted one by one, because everything affects everything. The problem was, having one organization try to do everything proved to be nearly impossible. The need to tap totally different areas of expertise, different funding streams, and different bureaucratic frameworks—just to mention a few—posed enormous barriers.

So the CDCs and other multi-dimensional entities tended to focus on economic development and housing, and sometimes health care and early child development, but stayed away from things like education. Governance and management of school systems tended to be located downtown and difficult to penetrate. Community control was tried here and there, most notably in New York City, but didn't stick. There were a few alternative schools in inner cities, but funding was hard to come by, and they mostly didn't survive.

Geoffrey Canada has embodied the idea of using education as an anchor for broader activities to help children and families—including early child development, parenting classes for new parents, and after-school enrichment. The Harlem Children's Zone, which Canada founded, came to be a multi-dimensional children's initiative through years of trial and error. Early on, his work was mainly focused on the off-school hours—using school buildings for after-school activities as part of New York City's Beacon Schools program, which opened schools throughout the city to nonprofit organizations.

As that effort progressed, Canada realized that there could be resonance in expanding the scale of the work to more parts of Harlem and to a broader age range, including dual-generation programs that would reach young parents and their children simultaneously. The final insight was that everything he was doing would be for naught if the schools the children attended were failing to teach them satisfactorily. For young people, the way out of the inner city is a good education that leads them to college or into the labor market.

The heart of the Harlem Children's Zone is the organization's charter schools. A recent evaluation praises the multi-dimensional design of the Zone's work but concludes that the key to lasting success is the schools. It may seem obvious, but it has taken a long time for people working on inner-city neighborhood revitalization to get the point that good schools have to be a cornerstone element of the strategy.

Why did it happen now? One reason is the advent of charter schools, which have made it possible to establish significant numbers of independent public schools in low-income neighborhoods. Before that, the public schools were in most places part of monolithic citywide systems that were virtually impervious to change implemented from the ground up. It is hard to see how the Zone could have been designed with schools as its central focus without the possibility of creating charter schools. Nonetheless, it should be said that, impelled by the competition of charter schools or not, public school systems have in recent years become more amenable to arrangements that reflect a greater commitment to parent- and community-sensitive values. Nor are charter schools a panacea. The work is to make all public schools exemplars of excellence. There are many problems with charter schools, but properly overseen, they should be part of a public-education reform strategy. For the Harlem Children's Zone, charter schools were a key building block.

The Harlem Children's Zone is not the only education-focused inner-city initiative. I mentioned Sandtown in Baltimore a little earlier. Here I am talking about the traditional public schools. I was impressed with the emphasis on the schools when I visited there in the late 1990s. I was fortunate in writing this book to have a chance to visit with Tina Hike-Hubbard, who has been working on education in the neighborhood since 1997 and is now the education director of Enterprise Community Partners and a member of the Baltimore City Board of School Commissioners. Hike-Hubbard was able to tell me how things have evolved based on her direct experience.

The Sandtown initiative itself—as a full-throttle effort to tackle all facets of life in Sandtown—no longer exists. Enterprise, James Rouse's organization, is best at doing affordable housing and associated community development. Community Building in Partnership, the nonprofit it created to drive the neighborhood improvement strategy, never took hold as a community institution and went out of business in 2008. Perhaps in part as a legacy to CBP's contribution, there are other vibrant actors in the community, especially New Song Church.

Enterprise has stayed energetically involved in housing and education. Its housing work has been quite successful. The economic status of the neighborhood as a whole hasn't changed much, but the housing that Enterprise and others have built or rehabilitated is stable. The purchasers and renters have stayed, and the foreclosure rate through the recession is very low. Enterprise built six hundred homes in the early 1990s. Those homes that were for sale sold for $58,500, with a $39,000 first mortgage. This was what has come to be called workforce housing—one had to have a job to get a mortgage. Buyers had incomes of $30,000 to $40,000 and were mainly people from the neighborhood who wanted to stay there. Only 15 percent have been sold to others over the past two decades. Over the years, the owners have finished the basements in the homes and made attractive improvements in the front and back yards. The blocks where they live are stable and livable. The people are where they want to be. It's a good story. The neighborhood isn't transformed, but it's much better for some of its residents.

The housing work is very important, but the education work is even more interesting because of the fact that it was truly pathbreaking when it started. And the fact that Tina Hike-Hubbard is now on the city's school board says a lot.

The story over the past dozen years is not only about the schools themselves but also about some ancillary activities that are very important. When I visited in 1999, the work was only in the elementary schools. Sylvia Peters, the charismatic woman who was then Tina Hike-Hubbard's boss, was frustrated that she and her colleagues couldn't crack the nearby middle school, where the gains they had made in the elementary schools were being destroyed.

Over the years, the local school became a K–8 school, so the Enterprise people were able to stay involved with the neighborhood schools through eighth grade. (Middle schools are being phased out citywide now.) As I write, Baltimore has a widely admired superintendent, Andres Alonso, so the citywide prospects are pretty good. Nonetheless, Hike-Hubbard says, the ups and downs of Pinderhughes, the middle school, have had more to do with facts on the ground in the building itself, especially the different principals who have been there. When I talked to her, she said there is another transition under way and "we have to make it work."

Having a well-connected person who works for a well-connected organization taking a special interest in a public school that serves low-income children is a good story in itself, but there is more to tell.

For one thing, Enterprise has a HIPPY home visiting program. HIPPY stands for Home Instruction for Parents of Preschool Youngsters. Founded in Israel, it was first brought to the United States by then-governor of Arkansas Bill Clinton. In Sandtown, Enterprise has a hundred families of three- to five-year-olds involved. Parents and grandparents do the visiting and bring twenty-seven books for parents to read to their children. They teach parents about lead safety, nutrition, and really any subject a parent asks about. Forty percent of the parents are in their teens, but some are as old as forty. One hundred percent of the children are passing state school readiness tests, a signal achievement.

Second, there is a community resource center located at the school. There are now nineteen such centers around the city, with a full-time staff person in each school. The staff person sees to getting glasses for kids, helping parents with jobs and job training and getting into GED programs, and arranging parent workshops.

Third, there is the Enterprise Women's Network that mentors girls in grades three through eight, ages seven through fourteen. They do field trips and educational workshops and travel outside the city to see green spaces. There are forty women involved—a very diverse group, young and old, black and white.

The City Heights Initiative in San Diego is another case where education became a major focus. Begun in 1994, Price Charities' work there was initially concerned with basic infrastructure and commercial development. The initiative started with construction: a shopping center and a community-friendly police substation that included a recreation center open to the public. The area had previously become a food desert with the closing of a local Safeway. The shopping center brought a new grocery store and a number of other stores selling at nationally competitive prices. The development efforts went on to include housing, an office center, a community health center, a library, three elementary schools, and a continuing-education facility—all situated to reinforce a sense of community. The police station and the shopping center are across the street from each other. Public drug use and public prostitution have disappeared.

The second phase was focused on partnering with nonprofits. The six-story office center that Price Charities built to house its own work became the locus for health care and social services. The La Maestra Clinic, a key health provider in the community, moved from a little house to a new facility financed by Price Charities and other partners. Tad Parzen, the executive vice president of Price Charities whose office is located in City Heights, says the clinic is exactly the same as the pediatric clinic his daughter goes to except that it lacks the flat-screen television and the tropical fish.

Price Charities' role has evolved from mainly being a funder into serving as an advocate, catalyst, deal maker, and convener, as well as a funder. Current projects are a new four-story all-purpose building that will have a Walgreens, a restaurant, and housing. More schools are on the way, too. Price hasn't financed all of these projects by itself. There are numerous other funders, both public and private, but Price's leadership and leveraged investment have been vital.

All along the way there has been a strong focus on education.

Education was a priority from the beginning in terms of physical development, but there is now a central emphasis on human-capital improvement too. In short, education is now a principal target. When they started working in City Heights, the schools were so bad that children were being sent by their parents to other schools around the city. Now there are eleven schools within one square mile. Price Charities is involved in academic enhancement, school-based health, and social work. Ninety percent of their activity now is in the schools, although strategically, Parzen says, they view the work not as narrowly education-related but as community-building.

Parzen says his biggest frustration is that they still have not been successful in getting people to stay in the neighborhood when their economic situation improves. For one thing, the community is still not safe at night, and in 2010 there were three murders in broad daylight near one of the schools. Public safety continues to be a challenge.

I would add one friendly amendment to the three education stories. We need to pursue racial desegregation wherever we can. This is not a legal point. Few discoverable instances of intentional segregation are still extant. Even the possibility of voluntary plans has been substantially truncated by the Supreme Court's 2007 decision regarding such plans in Seattle and Louisville. In addition, geography is the enemy in many places. That said, especially in medium-size cities, charters and magnets can produce at least modest oases of desegregation. We should pursue them wherever we can.

The Harlem Children's Zone, Sandtown, and City Heights stories are illustrative of multifaceted, community-based initiatives that focus on education as a key part of an attack on concentrated poverty. Not enough of the others are involved with education, but all such initiatives share a local combination of civic and philanthropic leadership and funding from an array of private and public sources. Finally creating a federal initiative that would provide serious resources to attack concentrated poverty remains an unfulfilled and perhaps unrealistic hope. In the meantime, the kind of local leadership that created the models we have is always a precious commodity to be greatly appreciated.

Jobs in the Regional Economy

In the mid-1990s, the Annie E. Casey Foundation began a program focused on getting inner-city residents hired for jobs throughout the regional economies of local areas. The endeavor began with six sites: Denver, Milwaukee, New Orleans, Philadelphia, St. Louis, and Seattle, although New Orleans fell by the wayside fairly quickly. It has proliferated to include some two hundred foundations that, along with public funds, support twenty-one sites around the country, all part of what is now called the National Fund for Workforce Solutions. In general, the local efforts are sector-specific partnerships that involve employers and unions in such areas as health care, technology, and construction. The partnerships include entities that do the necessary training and community-based organizations that identify prospects and offer mentoring and support during training, placement, and employment. They have made a difference, but, as in so many areas, the gains are measured more in the number of people who are doing better than in observable changes in the overall employment and poverty statistics. And much of the work is in jeopardy in the current wave of cutting public budgets.

The Casey program and the ensuing National Fund for Workforce Solutions are representative of an approach that deserves more public funding to enable wide replication: to give residents of the inner city a serious opportunity to be trained for, find, and hold on to jobs in the regional economy. There are community values in inner-city neighborhoods, at least among those with residents who have long-standing ties to the neighborhood. Better schooling in inner-city neighborhoods, combined with accessibility to jobs around the metropolitan area, offers the potential for transformative outcomes in those neighborhoods.

STRATEGIES FOR THE FUTURE

Researchers, practitioners, policy makers, and, most important, residents are still arguing vociferously over the right direction for inner-city policy. Nonetheless, there is an emerging view among a considerable number (including me) that the best approach is a pragmatic and holistic one: inner-city revitalization is important, but it must be an integrated part of a larger regional development strategy. Our goal should be to make it possible for people to live wherever they want in the metropolitan area and find jobs throughout the region, while also improving the livability of the neighborhoods where they live now. The key idea is that people should have real choices, and creating real choices means pursuing multiple policies and strategies simultaneously. This is the strategic frame. Moving forward is necessarily a long-term project.

Choice is controversial in more ways than one. To create residential choice throughout the region requires a new intensity in enforcing laws that prohibit all forms of relevant discrimination. Minorities moving to the suburbs still find themselves steered to same-race or same-ethnicity neighborhoods. Realtors, subtly or not, suggest that people looking for a new home will be most comfortable with people of their own race or ethnicity or class. Discrimination in the credit market is rampant, with creditworthy minorities still pushed regularly into subprime loans. And minorities encounter school districts' line-drawing policies in the suburbs that result in same-race and same-ethnicity schools.

Concerns of a different kind attend the question of making it possible for people to remain where they are in the inner city. These are likely to remain same-race neighborhoods. I do not believe in perpetuating racial segregation, even if it is technically not state-mandated segregation. Our priority should be policies that promote desegregation throughout metropolitan areas. But if strong steps are taken to help people improve their personal economic situation and the neighborhood around them as well, that will empower them to have the wherewithal to move out if they want to; if they stay in what turns into a healthier neighborhood, that will be their choice.

If people are to have choice about where they reside—in addition to the need for much more robust enforcement of antidiscrimination laws—there needs to be a ramped-up housing-supply policy in the realms of both public and affordable housing. It also means an increased investment in federally financed housing-choice vouchers that subsidize rents and let people choose where they will live, enriched with social services so people can use them effectively in the suburbs as well as in the city.

There is serious debate over the efficacy of policies to deconcentrate inner-city poverty. Studies of past efforts have shown mixed results. Nevertheless, central-city minorities have for decades been finding their way to what are now mixed-race and mixed-ethnicity inner-ring suburbs, sometimes with government help pursuant to litigation to desegregate public housing and sometimes with funding from a program created by Congress. The results are far from perfect, partly because of the policy failures mentioned above. But it makes sense that lower-income people can also succeed and provide better lives for their children in new surroundings if we take the measures necessary to encourage, subsidize, and otherwise facilitate their choices. What is needed is strategic thinking about a broader approach to housing choice throughout metropolitan regions.

The other side of the coin is the constellation of issues relating to those who would choose to remain in the inner city. I see six areas of action here. Operationally, these ideas have two strategic purposes: to build a stronger platform for those who would like to move out but don't currently have the capacity to do so and to strengthen the community for those whose choice it is to stay in the inner city.

One key aim has to be a strategy of pursuing a living income for everyone, derived as much as possible from work. This is a remedy that applies across the board, but it has a special resonance for those who want to stay in the inner city. Raising their incomes will make a major difference in the quality of life in the neighborhood. Policies such as the minimum wage, health coverage, affordable child care, excellent public education, help with the cost of housing and college, and a decent safety net are important for the whole society, but they have a particular relevance to breaking the back of concentrated poverty.

A second element is to do everything possible to help inner-city residents get and keep jobs in the regional economy. This means developing sector-specific partnerships among employers, schools, colleges, and community-based organizations to prepare people of all ages for good jobs that are projected to be most available in the coming years (and this is of course a challenge to the education community generally). It also means special attention to transportation, whether by mass transit or car, to enable inner-city residents to commute to their jobs wherever they are located. Of course, all of this can be done well or badly. Employers can distort job-training programs for their own narrow purposes, and proprietary trade schools can misuse public funds. Proper oversight has to be part of the equation.

Middle-skilled jobs offer promise in coming years and, as baby boomers retire, so does the possibility that green jobs will come to be a realistic source of work. If these opportunities are to reach everyone, specific mechanisms need to be in place to make that happen. The pathways should have initial on-ramps in high schools and community colleges—and also through nonprofit organizations like YouthBuild—that reach young people who are already disconnected from school and work and offer the education, training, and personal development support they need to get into the job market or pursue further education.

The third key is livable neighborhoods. Streets should be well-lit, parks and playgrounds conveniently located and attractive, and law enforcement effective and fair. The retail stores, cinemas, parks, playgrounds, and other amenities that people in every other neighborhood have should be available to people in low-income neighborhoods. The obvious synergistic point is that residents have to have the income necessary to support businesses located in the neighborhood. Quality health and child care facilities need to be accessible, too.

A fourth is that neighborhood schools should be of high quality and that school quality should be a part of an overall urban and antipoverty strategy, rather than siloed off by itself. School systems and educational innovators should make inner cities a preferential site for the establishment of innovative and high-quality schools, with charter schools being a useful part of a strategy for improving educational opportunities for children in high-poverty neighborhoods—desegregated racially wherever possible. Locating magnet schools in or near low-income neighborhoods is one strategy to attract a mix of income and racial backgrounds to the benefit of all. Improving schools and improving neighborhoods go hand in hand.

President Obama pledged in his campaign to take the Harlem Children's Zone nationwide with an initiative he calls Promise Neighborhoods. To that end, funding for twenty planning grants was appropriated during the first full year of his administration, followed by a modest expansion for a second year of operation. The number of applications for the planning grants was impressive but the pace of expansion has collided with the current political situation.

Nonetheless, Promise Neighborhoods represents an understanding, too long in coming, that any strategy to address concentrated poverty from a place-based perspective must have an emphasis on the education of the neighborhood's children. At the same time, it is important to understand that the Promise Neighborhoods idea offers new departures in only a limited number of places. An overall strategy to improve education for all low-income children, especially those in low-income neighborhoods, is the approach with much greater potential for broad-scale change.

Fifth, very important but not without risk to current residents who wish to remain in their neighborhoods, are efforts to attract higher-income people. Gentrification should be promoted, albeit carefully, and not impeded. Attracting people to the neighborhood who support its preservation as a mixed-income community would raise the median income of the area and, ultimately, lift the quality of life of everyone living there. But anti-displacement policies are essential. Tenants should have rights of first refusal to buy apartment buildings that landlords or developers want to convert to condominiums. Homeowners should be given circuit-breaker property tax relief so they aren't forced to sell due to unaffordable property taxes. Inclusionary zoning requiring developers to create new multiple dwellings and to make a reasonable fraction available on an affordable basis can be helpful. Public funds that invest in projects to develop and rehabilitate affordable housing must use their resources strategically to see that a fair share of the work occurs in inner-city neighborhoods, especially where the investment will contribute to enhancing the income mix in the area.

For more isolated neighborhoods with persistent and intergenerational poverty, it will be more difficult to attract new residents with higher incomes. But even in these neighborhoods, middle-income people could be enticed in better economic times by lower prices on attractive new housing. Of course, the neighborhood also has to be safe, have good schools, and offer parks and recreation and other amenities.

Sixth and finally, explicit attention to the behavioral patterns— denigration of the value of education, crime, nonmarital childbearing, and more—that have been associated with concentrated poverty is essential. Sad to say, they have become embedded and, in effect, intergenerational. The structural frameworks and continuing racism and racial discrimination have to be addressed, but so do the issues of personal and parental responsibility. Much of what is needed has to happen on the ground, in the community, carried out as a matter of civic action.

The essential premise for federal policy on concentrated urban poverty is that the necessary change must be comprehensive, with presidential leadership and, as necessary, legislation to involve every department and agency with responsibility for some relevant aspect of the task. The same is true for state and local government. The ostensibly overarching strategies of the past essentially let key players off the hook. This was true of Lyndon Johnson's Model Cities and Bill Clinton's Empowerment Zones. The task needs to be broken down into parts but connected to achieve the maximum collective impact. No one program can do everything that has to be done.

The education people have to pay attention to making the schools work — including co-location of and connection to health care facilities, child care, afterschool programs, and other social services. Transit agencies need to design the next generation of systems not just for suburban commuters entering the city but also for city residents headed for the suburbs. Housing policy needs to be regional and neighborhood-based. Energy policy needs to build "smart grids" and promote green jobs in the inner city and elsewhere. Environmental protection doesn't stop at the inner-city neighborhood line. Federal policy and funding will be needed to leverage much of what needs to be done.

We need to act on what we have learned about concentrated poverty. Bedford-Stuyvesant and other neighborhood revitalization initiatives were based on the premise that a poor area can be fixed by efforts within their borders, albeit with outside funding. There is no such thing as a neighborhood revitalization policy that can occur in isolation. For the twenty-first century, we must attack urban concentrated poverty with strategies that are regional in scope, as well as beneficial to people where they live now. Robert Kennedy had it right in the broad strokes if not in the exact details in his trilogy of speeches in 1966. Closing the last of the speeches, he said, "We are only at the beginning of the beginning in thinking about opportunities for all."[13] We know much more about the details now. No one in this nation should be part of any group that someone can rightly call "The Abandoned."

7

Young People: Improving the Odds

As some readers will know, my wife, Marian, is the founder and CEO of the Children's Defense Fund (CDF). One of the most beautiful things CDF does annually in seven cities around the country is to honor five high school seniors in each city who have beaten the odds and award them scholarships for college. CDF has been doing this for more than twenty years, so there are by now some seven hundred former honorees and the earliest ones are midway along in their professional careers.

These young men and women beat some really daunting odds. Most grew up in poverty. Most were victims of sexual or other serious abuse of some kind. Most had a parent who abused drugs or alcohol. Many were homeless along the way. Many spent time in foster care. Some witnessed a father physically attacking a mother. A few witnessed one parent killing the other.

What they have achieved is phenomenal. Many were the first in their family to go to college, and some were at the top of their class at the very best schools. They are now physicians and engineers and tenured professors at prestigious universities. Many are teachers in public schools. One in the very first group went to Harvard Medical School, and a 2010 honoree is studying electrical engineering at MIT. My wife thinks one may end up being president of Haiti. It is all truly amazing.

No matter how awful things are, some children are both wondrously resilient and incredibly talented. One way or another, they find their way to caring adults who mentor and support them and show them a path of possibility. Every time someone is there for a child who is at enormous risk and helps that child navigate a perilous voyage, it is worth celebrating.

This is all marvelous, but it is also infuriating and shameful. Because for every one of those children who makes it through against the odds, there are ten, twenty, a hundred, a thousand?—I don't know—who could have made it if they had had a fair chance. We will always need caring adults, but we also need schools that work, communities that work, and all the other support systems that give people the opportunity to succeed.

And when we talk about beating the odds, the odds aren't just the horrible homes that too many children endure. They are also the odds presented by terrible schools, the lure and danger of the streets, and the pipeline to prison. We definitely need to continue helping children one by one—it adds up to thousands and thousands—but we need to tackle the systemic issues, too.

A FEW WORDS ABOUT THE CURRENT SCHOOL REFORM DEBATE

One area where there is some hope—where the political factions typically at war with one another have been in at least some measure of agreement in recent years—is the importance of ensuring that all children have the opportunity to get a good education. It has been a long time in coming, and there is more than a little disagreement as to how to get there from here, but it's fair to say there is significant bipartisan support for school reform that will benefit, first and foremost, low-income children. Or was. The momentum for reform is seriously endangered by the massive teacher layoffs that have occurred during the recession. And I'm also worried that there is a dangerous acrimony developing—not in and of itself a partisan divide—that may have the effect of endangering the bipartisan agreement that has enabled useful reform to occur in a considerable number of states.

Two decades ago, it was hard to name a school system that one could genuinely say was pursuing a promising strategy for reform that would reach all children. Now there is a Broad Prize awarded to school systems for excellence in public education, especially urban public education. Such a prize, with substantial numbers of candidates every year, simply could not have existed twenty years ago. There would have been too few candidates. Two decades ago, there were no charter schools. Now there are many, some of which are unquestionably producing fabulous results. Two decades ago, Teach for America was just getting started. Now they have to rent the Washington Convention Center for their alumni convention.

There is indeed a genuine movement for change in the way we approach the education of low-income children in our country. The young people who went to Mississippi in 1964 have a twenty-first-century counterpart—the young people who have enlisted in the cause of school reform for the children who need it the most. Since the roots of the movement go back twenty years or more, the oldest of those young people are now running school systems and charter schools and working at high levels in the Obama administration. Those who came after are at it, too, as teachers and as staff for political and educational leaders at all levels. Others are advocates and academics and commentators. The field is vibrant.

I see it in my own family. Our son Josh has been a public school teacher, charter school principal, and a policy maker in two public school systems and now works on education at the Gates Foundation. Our son Jonah founded and runs Stand for Children, which has become an important advocacy force for school reform across the country. They are the twenty-first-century counterpart to the Freedom Summer activists in Mississippi. (Our son Ezra is a fabulous sports documentary filmmaker.)

My main purpose in this chapter is to discuss the education young people must have in order to qualify for the jobs of the future that I talked about in an earlier chapter, especially the role that career- and job-related education should play in keeping inner-city young people in school and creating more pathways to productive adulthood.

First, though, I want to say a word about an overarching issue. It is about the strategic balance between excellent education and poverty reduction.

There is a debate going on that reflects what I think is a false dichotomy between some school reformers and some antipoverty advocates. One "side," particularly concerned that too many teachers over the years have thrown up their hands and said that poor children bring too much baggage to school and cannot be taught, stresses (correctly, in my view) that every child can learn. The other, believing (also correctly) that maximum success must also entail poverty reduction, puts its stress on the need to emphasize poverty reduction along with school reform.

This is not a real debate, as I see it. On the one hand, we now have the evidence from high-performing charter schools and traditional public schools that "all children can learn" is not just a bumper sticker. Many schools are doing a remarkable job of transforming the lives of low-income children. On the other hand, we know much more from neuroscience and developmental psychology about how children's brains develop and the gaps in development that are evident as of age three when low-income children do not receive the same stimuli that other children get routinely.[1] And we know that children who have lived in poverty and are not reading proficiently by third grade are about three times as likely not to graduate from high school as those who have never been poor.[2]

There is no basis for any school reformer to give up on the work of improving education because the pace of reducing poverty is too slow. Schools can be a driver for change in and of themselves. At the same time, placing health clinics and community resource centers in schools, improving nutrition, and advocating for the expansion of early childhood programs and parental support efforts are all very important, are eminently achievable, and will make a difference in children's lives.

But that is not enough. We cannot forget the underlying issues of jobs and income and the closely connected and still-important issues of race and gender. The poverty-related activities that can be conducted within schools and by using schools as a base are worthwhile, but people should not confuse them with the policies that are necessary to reduce poverty meaningfully. Quality education is a core strategy in fighting poverty, but unless we fight poverty on all fronts, the schools will not succeed in helping all children have the chance to achieve their full potential.

LOSING ONE GENERATION AFTER ANOTHER: WHEN WILL WE STOP THE CARNAGE?

Many who read this book will be thoroughly familiar with the terminology and the reality of the cradle-to-prison pipeline. The overincarceration of African American and Latino young men is a national scandal. Low-income young men of color—especially those growing up in high-poverty neighborhoods—are fated under current circumstances to end up in prison in percentages that far exceed their share of the population.[3] I saw this happening in the late 1970s when I was head of the youth corrections agency in New York State, and it has gotten much, much worse since then. We are losing generation after generation.

Check the boxes: father in and out of prison or whereabouts unknown or never known. Mother struggling to find steady work and often not succeeding. Drugs or alcohol in the parental picture somewhere. Violence in the home. Early childhood inattention or worse. Terrible schools. No caring adult other than the mother or grandmother in the boy's life. Street culture that valorizes defiance and denigrates educational achievement. Police all too willing to arrest.

Result: time in prison, likely fathering children and not marrying the mother, and difficulty in finding work for the rest of his life. Poverty in· childhood makes these young men strong candidates for getting into trouble with the law in the first place, and time in prison makes them even stronger candidates for lives of poverty and disenfranchisement from the democratic process, pushing the arithmetic of politics to the right and shrinking the constituency for support of low-income communities.

Not all boxes apply to each young man, of course, but enough do. Whether the underlying facts are George W. Bush's "soft bigotry of low expectations" or Michelle Alexander's *The New Jim Crow*, which brilliantly describes the targeting of young black men in the criminal justice system[4]—and both ideas are operative— the situation is truly dire. Comprehensive reform of the juvenile and criminal justice systems, including our misbegotten "war on drugs," is a must.

Dire as it is, though, the cradle-to-prison pipeline is comparatively narrow. There is a wider pipeline yet. I call it the cradle-to-nowhere pipeline, and it is full of girls as well as boys. There are 804,100 youth and young adults (ages eighteen to twenty-nine) in prison or jail,[5] and about 92.4 percent of them are men.[6] But there are 3 million or more youth and young adults who are not in school and are out of work for a long time, most of whom will not spend time in jail or prison.[7] (Andrew Sum of Northeastern University puts the number as high as 5.2 million.[8])

These young people have come to be called "disconnected." Depending on the estimate involved, they constitute from one in twelve up to as many as one in six of the sixteen- to twenty-four-year-old age group.[9] About one-third are parents, approximately fifty thousand are homeless, and many have lived for long periods of time in foster care.[10] If nothing changes, at least half of these 3 million young people will spend much of their lives unemployed or sporadically and marginally employed at best. Not surprisingly, African American, Latino, and Native American young people are disproportionately represented among the disconnected.

Three million disconnected youth is a number that was in wide currency before the Great Recession. It includes some high school graduates, because young people who do not pursue postsecondary education or training face increasingly impassable pathways into the legal labor market. The pathway is even less reliable for disconnected youth who do not graduate from high school. Only about two-thirds of all students—and only half of all African Americans, Latinos, and Native Americans—who enter ninth grade graduate with regular diplomas four years later.[11] For minority males, the figures are even lower. And dropping out is disastrous. In 2000, when unemployment was comparatively low, 50 percent of high school dropouts were employed, compared to 93 percent of adults holding an associate's degree or better.[12] It's a lot worse than that now.

You can see a dropout factory in process if you go to any inner-city neighborhood on a school day. You will see young people on the street who clearly should be in school. Some of them are headed for the kind of trouble that means jail. More of them are headed basically nowhere. Why aren't they in school? Basically, they don't see any payoff from staying there. They don't see anything offered in school that leads anywhere they see as realistic. Some of them will say that nobody knows or cares whether they come to school or not (and too many of them are right). Some of them can't read or write or do math very well but have been passed along from year to year anyway. Nearly all of them have heard messages of disrespect for education on the street, in the music they listen to, and even at home. They are shooting themselves in the foot, but everything they hear and see reinforces the idea that they have no future.

Some of those we'll find on that street corner are there because the school told them to stay away. We have heard for years of the excesses of zero-tolerance policies. Recently, a study done by the Council of State Governments Justice Center and Texas A&M University's Public Policy Research Institute provided a quantum leap in the concrete evidence. The researchers looked at 6.6 million student records for three classes of Texas seventh-graders and tracked them for six years or more. Nearly 1 million instances of discipline sanctions were found. Schools with similar profiles had widely disparate discipline policies. More than 97 percent of disciplined students were sanctioned for "discretionary" infractions,

mainly classroom disruption and insubordination; less than 3 percent of the cases were state-mandated offenses such as bringing
weapons or drugs to school. African Americans had a 31 percent
higher chance of being suspended for a "discretionary" offense
than whites and Hispanics.[13] And 23 percent of students who were
suspended at least once had contact with the juvenile justice system, compared to just 2 percent of students with no suspensions.
The best policy is not to use suspensions profligately in the first
place, which the evidence shows is the successful policy of many
schools, because the evidence also shows a pattern of progressively
greater alienation once the repetition begins. So school discipline
policies have a lot to do with the pipelines we're talking about.

What should we be doing about all of this? Early childhood development, competent teaching from kindergarten on, and so on,
but what about high school? Is the answer college for all?

Here we wade into a debate that has been going on at least since
Booker T. Washington and W.E.B. Du Bois. Basically, every high-
performing academic high school articulates its main goal as going to college. There have been some spectacular successes, and
I have no interest in arguing with the approach they use. It works
for them.

But it is not a shoe that fits everyone, even at those schools.
If you look a little closer at many of the graduates of good high
schools that serve low-income students, you will see that a number
of students go on to community colleges and may or may not obtain a bachelor's degree. You will see that some who don't get a BA
do get a diploma or certification to pursue a productive career that
doesn't require a four-year degree. College for all may be the flag
they fly, but the outcomes—and I mean the good outcomes—are
more varied.

The stakes are highest at large public inner-city high schools—
the dropout factories that are scarring so many lives. The first task is
to get students' attention, to convince them to stick around. Inner-
city high schools should offer motivated students a full opportunity
to go to as good a college as they can get in to, but students also need

options that are more tangible, more hands-on, and more immediately rewarding than the promise of an education that leads one to a rich life of the mind. Of course, some young people will thrive on a liberal education regardless of their background, and some young people resonate with a more hands-on option wherever they grow up. Young people of all economic strata flock to good career- and technical-education programs in suburban schools. But it is especially important that there be strong career pathways in inner-city high schools. We don't want to reinvent the dysfunctional vocational education of the twentieth century, and we don't have to. Vocational High School in Minneapolis, where I grew up, was a dumping ground. We don't want to go back there.

What we want in the twenty-first century is a system that gives young people a sense of effect and reward—that if they do try, they can get a job and lead a life they desire. They need to see an achievable road map toward a successful adult life.

To that end, high schools in general, but especially inner-city high schools, should offer educational options that are specifically career-oriented. The twenty-first-century version should open the door to entry-level jobs, but also to further education that could lead to the highest degree in a field. A person who enters a health-careers high school program should be able to graduate and get a job as a technician or an aide and then go back to school or go right on to college—maybe beginning with community college to become a licensed practical nurse or more specialized technician, and then going on later to pursue further degrees. The program in high school should involve hands-on experience in the workplace—preferably for pay—that is tangible and immediately rewarding. The more flexibility, the better.

This flexibility, by the way, has been hugely helpful to immigrants in particular. It is an advantage that the United States has over European systems like Germany that track heavily. More than other countries, we are the land of many second choices, and this is a key for disadvantaged groups.

There seems to be a pitched battle going on about approaches like the one I just laid out. Critics say this sort of approach is condescending, or it's racist, or it's classist. We had the same argument in 1971 when I went to work at the University of Massachusetts. A bunch of very well-meaning Harvard PhDs had been hired around 1968 or so to staff a new Boston campus for the university. The entire curriculum was liberal arts. No other options.

"How about a college of public and community service?" we said. "How about a college of finance and administration?"

Answer: "No. Never. Over our dead bodies. We are bringing to working-class people the same education that people get at Harvard." They said, "That's the way of democracy. Your way is paternalism."

"Your colleges are wonderful," we responded, "but the graduates need to feed their families. Let's at least offer some curricular options that lead to jobs."

We did create the two new colleges and everything went well.

Career and Technical Education (CTE) is the twenty-first-century version of vocational education. It exists all over the country, although its quality in inner-city high schools is still too often the old vocational education of my youth in Minneapolis even if the terminology has changed. Coupled with and closely connected to community colleges, CTE, if done well, is a viable option for helping disconnected youth make a successful transition to adulthood. Quality career- and technical-education programs connect high school students to the world of work and put some on a path to earn an occupational certificate straight out of high school. But they also require students to complete coursework for admission to a four-year college. This kind of high school curriculum is based on a realistic assessment of the American economy, as jobs that require an associate's degree or comparable certificate are the ones that are projected to grow the fastest in the coming years.

The U.S. Bureau of Labor Statistics projected that total employment will increase by 15.3 million jobs over the decade ending in 2018, and the total number of new and replacement jobs over that period will be 47 million, according to the Georgetown Center on Education and the Workforce. Nearly two-thirds of those jobs will require at least some postsecondary education, while people with no more than a high school degree will fill just 37 percent of the job openings, just half the percentage of jobs they held in the early 1970s.[14] About a third of the jobs will be the "middle-skill jobs"[15] that I discussed earlier—for example, construction managers, police officers, paralegals, and dental hygienists. These are good jobs. In fact, 27 percent of people with postsecondary licenses or certificates—credentials short of an associate's degree—earn more than the average bachelor's degree recipient.[16]

President Obama and Education Secretary Arne Duncan have tried to move in the right direction, at least in part. The president's American Graduation Initiative for community colleges—which was only partially funded—was premised on hard thinking about the jobs coming down the road and the preparation that is needed for people to be able to take on those jobs. On the other hand, it did not focus enough attention on students who need remediation or other extra help in order to succeed and, even more important, career-oriented education at the high school level has received surprisingly little attention in an administration that has focused more attention on the education of low-income children than any in history.

Now, of course, neither the Obama administration nor states and localities are in a position to put new money into anything. Programs including the Perkins Act, which funds vocational education, were pared down in the budget cutting of 2011, and more cuts are on the way both nationally and locally. We won't see nearly enough change until we stop starving our schools.

Career and Technical Education

We are not starting from a clean slate here. We can learn from models that have been evaluated positively and others that have impressive track records.

Career Academies, which have been around for some four

decades and are evaluated rigorously, are perhaps the leading example of what should be available to inner-city students and low-income students everywhere. They exist in about 2,500 high schools around the country. They combine academic college-oriented study with career and technical courses, organized around career themes. The model encompasses up to sixteen career clusters in such areas as health, business and finance, and computer technology. Students get hands-on experience in the course of their learning by participating in volunteer projects at actual workplace locations. The work-based learning and one-on-one features of the academies are a key factor in their success. On the other hand, the quality of career academies, like CTE generally, varies from school to school, with much too high an incidence of poor quality in inner-city high schools, where the mere title of "career academy" is no guarantee of instructional quality.

A particular Career Academy network that is notably successful is the National Academy Foundation network of high schools. Located in forty states and the District of Columbia, it serves nearly fifty thousand students in almost five hundred academies located at four hundred schools. Its clientele is disproportionately African American and Latino. The network has four focus areas: finance, IT, engineering, and hospitality and tourism. Industry partnerships are key to the process. These schools have a 90 percent graduation rate, and 52 percent of their students go on to receive BAs.[17] Key factors in their success are paid internships, volunteer classroom teaching by business partners, and one-on-one mentoring.

The Manpower Demonstration Research Corporation's evaluation of Career Academies yielded impressive results. The strongest and most pervasive differences were found among students at highest risk of school failure. Among this subgroup, the academy students attended school more regularly, earned more course credits, were more likely to participate in extracurricular activities and volunteer projects, and were less likely to be arrested.[18] As of spring of their senior year, the dropout rate for the high-risk group was reduced from 32 percent in the control group to 21 percent among the Career Academy students.[19] Male participants earned an average of over $2,500 a year more on average than nonpartici-pants four years after graduating.[20] Eight years after graduating, the academy graduates had earned a cumulative $30,000 more than non-participants.[21]

Massachusetts has also been at the forefront of vocational-technical education (VTE). Every student in the state has access to a VTE program. VTE students have substantially better graduation rates than the regular high schools (90.5 percent vs. 80.9 percent) and higher state test scores, too.[22] The Massachusetts Business Alliance for Education reports that VTE graduates are more job-ready than other high school graduates.

The sixty-three VTE schools are in essence large magnet schools. Half of a student's instructional time is spent in shop or career education. Along with traditional trades such as carpentry, cosmetology, and plumbing, VTE schools offer telecommunica-tions, computer repair, medical assistance, environmental tech-nology, and pre-engineering. A standard part of the VTE school experience is the "co-op" for seniors, where they work for pay at a real job in their field of study.[23]

There are other examples of good programs and individual schools that are models of what I have described. High Schools That Work is another model and is now used in 1,200 schools in thirty-two states. The Linked Learning Initiative in California is yet another, which has been adopted by eleven school districts in the state. So there are numerous exemplars. But we face an im-portant challenge in this area. High-quality CTE is a key building block in a strategy to tackle the horrible graduate rates of inner-city high schools. Of course, a traditional, huge, impersonal inner-city high school faces multiple challenges that go far beyond CTE. But my sense is that too few cities think of quality CTE as an important tool in efforts to prevent dropping out of school and to start young people on a path to a good job in the twenty-first-century economy.

Community Colleges

The next piece of the pathway is postsecondary education, especially community college. The community college is the key institution to prepare people of all ages for the jobs of the future. The good jobs that will be available (and I'm still worried that there won't be enough of them) require postsecondary education, sometimes a two-year degree and in other cases a certificate of some sort.

The community college is America's second-chance institution. With all of the concerns about what we don't do well enough, one thing we do well in contrast to almost every other country with an advanced economy is to offer a second chance. Typically, other nations test early and track young people almost irrevocably at a young age, often even before they are in their teens. In the United States, the community college is a place—the primary place—where people can make up for poor past performance, pick up where they left off, or change course from their previous career.

So the community college is America's melting pot—not only in its immense student diversity, but especially in the age range of its students. It is a place to start a postsecondary education immediately after high school and a place to come back to for more education at any age. In constructing a framework of off-ramps and on-ramps going back and forth from school to work and work to school, the community college is the linchpin. It is the flexible institution where people can start and stop and start again, go at their own pace, attend full time or part time, and time their continuing education or training so they can move to the next rung on a career ladder.

One unfortunate fact, more evident now than ever, is that we don't have enough seats at community colleges to meet the demand. Unemployed people and others seeking to upgrade their skills are spiking the demand, and fierce budget cuts in many states are limiting the supply of seats. Proprietary colleges have stepped into the breach. Some are effective (although expensive), but far too many range from less than good to altogether fraudulent. One simple challenge as we emerge from the recession is to increase our commitment to community colleges.

Beyond that, we need a particular intensification of our efforts to reach young people coming out of high schools with high-poverty student bodies, including those who have not graduated.

A favorite model of mine, which began at Portland Community College in Portland, Oregon, is Gateway to College. Gateway to College, now in thirty colleges in sixteen states, is a second-chance model for high school dropouts. The community college establishes a high school on its campus. Through dual credit, the students in the program earn a high school diploma and an average of thirty-five college credits, and then move seamlessly into the college itself.

Gateway students are initially placed into small learning communities during their first term and take classes together in reading, writing, math, and college skills. They then move on to taking classes with the general student population. They receive one-on-one advising and support throughout the program.

Whatever remediation the students need in order to be ready for college work is provided while the students are in the high school. The high school is funded under the public school funding formula, so students do not use up Pell Grant funds for their high school diploma or remediation. At too many other community colleges, remediation often devours a disturbingly big chunk of Pell Grant funds. This is very important. Many students who have high school diplomas but are ill-prepared for college-level coursework wind up in remedial classes but then drop out without ever earning a single college credit.

Fifty-two percent of all Gateway students who complete one term earn a high school diploma. The success of the program is remarkable because the average previous high school grade point average of the students is 1.6. Having struggled with poor attendance in high school, Gateway students have an average attendance of

81 percent.[24] Most of the students are from low-income and minority homes and will be the first in their families to go to college.

Gateway to College is a fabulous model and should be replicated far more extensively (with the cautionary note that competent implementation is critical—some current sites are more impressive than others).

A similar model is the College, Career and Technology Academy, conducted in partnership with South Texas College. Jobs for the Future, an organization that studies work-related issues regarding young people, conducted a fifty-state survey of programs that integrate high school and college for youth who fall off the track. Through CCTA, former dropouts complete their high school diplomas and smoothly transition into college courses when they are ready. They can begin college courses while finishing their high school requirements. CCTA's design allows young people to experience themselves as college students rather than high school dropouts. The design is easily replicable, and several neighboring areas in the state have launched their own versions, recognizing the boost this can give their graduation rates. The per-pupil cost is actually lower than that of a traditional high school, despite the smaller class sizes, because of savings on nonacademic expenditures like sports and clubs.[25]

Reaching Dropouts Down the Road

Young adults who have made big mistakes can turn their lives around when offered the chance to learn, work, and contribute to society. A recent analysis by Jobs for the Future of data from the National Education Longitudinal Study found that nearly 60 percent of high school dropouts eventually earned their high school diploma.[26] If that's the good news, the bad news is that 40-plus percent did not. We need to do much more to create a system to help struggling youth to become productive members of society.

The question of reconnection depends on the age of the youth and whether there is a particular issue associated with the disconnection beyond having dropped out of school. Reconnection poses special challenges for four groups for whom our rhetoric of concern far exceeds the magnitude of our action: youth in the juvenile or criminal justice system; young, unmarried mothers; adolescents in foster care; and homeless youth. A traditional school might or might not work for young people in any of those circumstances. If the nature of their disconnection is associated with being strongly alienated from a traditional school, an alternative arrangement is in order.

If the youth is too old for the K–12 system, other options are essential. Promising models for older youth and young adults typically provide opportunities to learn work-related and technical skills while earning a diploma, and include paid work several days a week. In this realm nonprofits have to play a major role—often tied to community colleges—in addition to the workplace itself. The new Adult Charter School for seventeen- to twenty-four-year-olds that is part of the Maya Angelou family of schools in Washington, D.C., is another promising idea. And Job Corps is a program with a track record of nearly half a century and still going strong.

YouthBuild is a personal favorite of mine. It is a brilliant organization serving young people ages sixteen through twenty-four. It's also a double entendre: it builds the youth themselves, and it builds affordable housing for low-income and homeless people. It emphasizes leadership development, ethics, and serving and building the community. Its participants have built twenty thousand housing units since 1994, and a hundred thousand young people have been involved since then.[27]

Founded by Dorothy Stoneman, a genuine genius (as well as one anointed by the MacArthur Foundation), YouthBuild has a long history in different forms and under different names over Dorothy's long career. Its current iteration goes back two decades or so to when Dorothy convinced Senator John Kerry to advocate that the program be federally funded (along with funding from state and local governments and private sources). With the support of Senator Kerry and others in Congress, Dorothy has built a large and impressive organization.

On the other hand, it is a prime example of the disproportionate emphasis on cutting funds for domestic discretionary programs, which are a small slice of the overall budget but the first and most immediate target for the ax. Dorothy has proven that young people who have already had a strike or two against them can succeed. Nonetheless, their federal support will be targeted for cuts every year as long as today's political climate persists.

There were 4,252 young people in the program in 2010, and 18,000 were turned away.[28] Before the budget-cutting extravaganza started in 2011, there were 273 YouthBuild programs in forty-five states, the District of Columbia, and the Virgin Islands.[29] The sum of the budget cuts in 2011 and 2012 will leave one hundred of those programs without federal funding.[30] Most will survive (some on a scaled-back basis) through other funding sources, and some may well close their doors.

YouthBuild's participants are all poor when they come to the program, and 94 percent have not graduated from high school or gotten a GED. They are 71 percent male. They are 54 percent African American, 22 percent white, 20 percent Latino, and a small number are Native American or Asian American. Thirty-one percent are parents. Forty-three percent have been in the juvenile justice or criminal justice system. Forty-five percent were on some form of public assistance, and 19 percent had lived in public housing. The average age is 19.6 with a seventh-grade reading level.[31] The youth stay in the program for six to twenty-four months. Seventy-eight percent finish the program, 60 percent get jobs (at an average wage of $9.20) or go back to school, and 63 percent earn their GED.

We should not give up on anyone who wants to find his or her way to full participation in our society. YouthBuild is not for everyone—it is somewhat more male-oriented than female-oriented, for example—but it could serve thousands more people than it does. It would of course be better to reduce the flow of youth who become disconnected, but a full strategy to deal with the pipelines must include those who were not reached earlier. That is what YouthBuild is about. To say the least, it is deeply disturbing that young people who could make the most of a second chance will not get it because of today's politics.

Another important organization in the second-chance space is the Corps Network, which is the contemporary descendent of the New Deal Civilian Conservation Corps. The 158 Service and Conservation Corps that are the Network's constituency operate in forty-six states and involve 33,000 participants and 265,000 additional volunteers each year, with annual support from all sources of $549 million.[32] The Corps members, many of whom are AmeriCorps participants, work largely on conservation and clean-energy projects. Most of the participants are young people who were disconnected when they joined and are pursuing a second chance through their experience with the Corps.

Year Up is one of the many local programs around the country that work with young people who need a leg up, most of which receive no public funding. Year Up has been rigorously evaluated and comes out with flying colors. Founded in 2000, it now operates in eleven cities with a hundred corporate partners, serving low- and moderate-income young people eighteen to twenty-four. It is a "career first" program for high school graduates—disproportionately minorities—who have not yet had any postsecondary education. The one-year program is divided into a classroom and an internship phase. The first half includes training in technical skills, classes in writing and communications, instruction in professional skills, and an opportunity to earn college credits. The second half is an internship with top local companies. Over its decade-plus history, Year Up has placed more than 2,300 young people in internships, and 84 percent either obtain a job at an average $15-an-hour wage or go to college.[33]

A notable program was unveiled by New York City mayor Michael Bloomberg during the summer of 2011. In what is perhaps the most visible recognition by a major city of the crisis among low-income minority young men, Mayor Bloomberg pledged $30 million of his own money over the next three years to work on the "Young Men's Initiative," matched by an equal pledge from billionaire George Soros and funding from the city, for a total of $127 million.

The Bloomberg initiative includes job-recruitment centers in public housing, reorganizing probation efforts to make them more accessible in neighborhoods, establishing new fatherhood classes, and job-training programs that combine morning classes in math and literacy with paid internships in the afternoon. Public schools would refocus career-counseling efforts on high-risk youth beginning in middle school and intensify assessment of schools' success in serving African American and Latino males.[34]

Forty million dollars a year won't do the whole job, but it is not insubstantial, and the program has many of the elements I have discussed in this chapter. Instead of throwing up his hands and saying "intractable," as so many do, Mayor Bloomberg has acknowledged the crisis and taken steps to confront it. Private philanthropy is not the answer in and of itself, but it can create models for public investment to follow. We need both public and private investment and commitment.

We do not lack people who care, but we don't have enough of them. Nor do we lack public funding, but we don't have enough of that either. The federal investment in youth employment has actually declined over the past twenty-five years, from $1.5 billion in 1984 to $828 million in 2012, and that is without a correction for inflation.[35] (The 1984 appropriation would be $3.27 billion in today's dollars.) The Deficit Control Act of 2011 implies more cuts are on the way. So a fair question is to ask how the successful and promising models I have discussed can be brought to scale. One answer is that whatever scale we can achieve will appropriately come from a variety of sources: governments at all levels, businesses and foundations, individual giving, and the work of volunteers, depending on the particular program or initiative. Among other things, ending the expensive and unnecessary incarceration of young people would free up resources that could be used much more productively on behalf of young people at risk. The underlying challenge is to change public attitudes to place greater value on the lives of these young people.

The problem with our underinvestment in children who need extra attention begins when they are born and continues throughout, so it is not possible to say that one dereliction is worse than another. And it is of course true that a more effective investment in the early years, if kept up, would prevent many of the negative outcomes that come to pass later on. But when we see the problems that our earlier inattention has brought, we tend to say, "Oh, sorry, too late, too bad, it's over, there's nothing we can do now." It is unacceptable that we would shut our eyes to the young people, now almost grown up, we can still reach.

Education and child development—investing in our future— are a major piece of an antipoverty strategy. The totality of what we need to do for children would fill a shelf of books. My special passion for forty years—from Robert Kennedy through my work at the University of Massachusetts and particularly my time as the director of the New York State Division for Youth—has been the perilous voyage from adolescence to adulthood for those young people who face an especially rough passage. Ending poverty in America requires action on many fronts, but providing every young person the opportunity to be a full participant in our society could not be more important.

CONCLUSION

America is different in a lot of good ways from the time when I got started. We have made a great deal of progress in many areas that affect poverty—on race, on gender, on the creation of a medical safety net and a food safety net, on the economic security of the elderly. Optimists that we were in the continuing postwar glow of the 1960s, we may even have taken those things somewhat for granted when they happened. There is more to be done on each, but we have done well.

But then there were the things that we didn't foresee: the shift of the economy to so much low-wage work, the changes in family composition, the crisis in public education, the weakening of social mobility, the cradle-to-prison pipeline, the disconnection of so many young people from school and work.

We did a lot about poverty, to the point where there would be something like 40 million more people in poverty now without such things as food stamps, the Earned Income Tax Credit, and the indexing of Social Security to inflation.

Despite the damage done to the safety net under President Reagan and the demise of welfare under President Clinton, events that would have made poverty much worse were neutralized, even though not overcome, by the policies we enacted over the years. So if you look objectively at what has happened, the claim that nothing works is revealed for what it is—totally hot air.

But we need to be crystal clear now. We are headed in the wrong direction. The hole we are in is getting deeper and deeper. The costs of not doing the right thing now for all of our children are going to get higher and higher. The tents of Occupy Wall Street may be gone by the time this book appears, but "We are the 99%" remains. We have to act, for all of the 99 percent.

As long as middle-income voters think they have more in common with the people at the top than the people at the bottom, we are cooked. The question of jobs that produce enough income so people can live comfortably is an issue that cuts across a huge swath of the population. The question of how to deliver quality (and, after high school, affordable) education so that everyone is prepared for the best job they have the capacity to hold is an issue that confronts a substantial majority. The challenge is to get people in the middle to understand which side of the line they are on. If they continue to believe that social mobility is realistically available for themselves and their children the way things are playing out, they will be much less likely to do what they have to do to protect themselves, let alone sympathize with people down the line. The people have the power if they will use it, but they have to see that it is in their interest to do so.

In a way we have not seen since the Great Depression, the rich and the powerful are adding every day to the bricks that make up the wall of their separation from everyone else. The banks earn record profits but do not lend, and the government does not press them to do it. The big companies stockpile enormous cash reserves but do not hire, and the government does not stimulate demand for their products. And the answer to the possibility of raising taxes at the top just to the level they were a dozen years ago remains a resounding no.

This is crazy.

The first thing we need to do is roll back the Bush tax cuts for the wealthy. If we can't do that, we're not going to have the resources to do the next ten things. Attacking inequality means action at the bottom as well as the top. The fundamental and continuing priorities are jobs that yield a decent income, a reliable safety net, and an educational system that delivers for every child. The immediate priority, along with action on the revenue side, is to defend and protect the basic programs without which poverty would be even worse. And the most pressing need, in pure humanitarian terms, is to repair the rip in our American safety net that leaves us with so many millions who are in deep poverty, especially the 6 million people who have no income other than food stamps.

We should not kid ourselves. There is no inevitability to things remaining even as good as they are now. The wealth and income of the top 1 percent grows at the expense of everyone else. Money breeds power, and power breeds more money. It is a truly vicious circle.

Our side has one main weapon: people power. We need the public intellectuals and the advocates and the foundations and whichever powerful people are on our side. But our real weapon, our best weapon—our weapon of mass construction when we use it—is us. As I write, people seem to be waking up and emerging from their unaccountable passivity of the past two-and-a-half years. In Ohio, they rejected the governor's effort to destroy public unions. In Maine, they fought off a dangerous voter-protection law. In Mississippi, they turned away an anti-abortion proposition that was beyond the fringe. We can hope, but it will take a lot of work.

I have seen both the days of promise and the days of darkness, and I've seen them more than once. All history is like that. There have been times when it looked like the rich had a chokehold, irrevocably, on all of our resources and political power. They didn't last. There have been times when it looked like those who think the poor are poor simply because they made bad choices were in power permanently. They didn't last either.

We have to be at it steadily, all the time. This means both electoral politics and outside advocacy and organizing. We tend to lurch back and forth. My take on the Obama election in 2008 is that we put all our eggs in the electoral basket and then figured he would do it all and we could go about our business. There were two problems with that. One, he needed our help to get things done, and two, he needed to hear our voice about what he was not doing that he should have been doing and what he was doing that was wrong. You can't just vote and then disappear for four years. But there have also been times when we turned up our nose at the electoral part of it on some dopey theory that it didn't matter who won and found out otherwise, to our detriment. So one lesson, which we seem to learn and then forget over and over again, is that we have to work both the inside and the outside—in the electoral world and from the outside to keep elected officials honest and make them better than they would otherwise be.

I am an optimist. I have to be or I wouldn't have written this book.

ACKNOWLEDGMENTS

Thanks first to André Schiffrin, Ellen Adler, and The New Press for their interest in my writing this book. I'm very grateful to my research assistants—Austin Davidson, Marnie Kaplan, and Patrick Kane—for their great work and to Greg Kaufmann for his terrific help and support. Enormous thanks to Jason DeParle, who read and reread the manuscript and offered incredibly comprehensive and helpful suggestions. Special thanks, too, to David Super, Harry Holzer, Arloc Sherman and colleagues at the Center on Budget and Policy Priorities, Larry Mishel, Heather Boushey, Tom Kingsley, Jane Dimyan-Ehrenfeld, Lisa Pritchard-Bayley, David Birenbaum, Michael Wald, Mark Angney, and Josh and Jonah Edelman for educating me when I needed some intellectual nurturance and reading some or all of the book in draft. And thanks to Tina Hike-Hubbard, Chickie Grayson, Kelly Cartales, and Tad Parzen for taking the time to talk with me. Thanks also to Dean Bill Treanor and Associate Dean Robin West of Georgetown Law Center for the school's support of my research and writing, and to Kathryn Ticknor for her cheerful assistance in so many ways. Finally and always, I thank my dear wife, Marian, for her constant inspiration.

NOTES

1. A Snapshot of Our Current Mess

1. Jason DeParle and Robert M. Gebeloff, "Living on Nothing but Food Stamps," *New York Times*, January 3, 2010.

2. U.S. Department of Agriculture, "FY 2010 Allotments and Deduction Information," September 10, 2010, www.fns.usda.gov/snap/government/FY11_Al lot_Deduct.htm.

3. Food Research and Action Center, "SNAP/Food Stamp Monthly Participation Data," May 2011, frac.org/reports-and-resources/snapfood-stamp -monthly-participation-data/.

4. U.S. Department of Health and Human Services, "TANF—Caseload Data," May 26, 2011, www.acf.hhs.gov/programs/ofa/data-reports/caseload/caseload_cur rent.htm.

5. *Duplication, Overlap, and Inefficiencies in Fed. Welfare Programs: Hearing Before H. Comm. on Oversight and Gov't Reform, Subcomm. on Regulatory Affairs, Stimulus Oversight and Gov't Spending*, 112th Cong. (2011).

2. What We Have Accomplished

1. Lyndon Johnson, "Remarks upon Signing the Economic Opportunity Act," August 20, 1964, 1963–64 Public Papers, part 2, p. 988.

2. Arloc Sherman, "Safety Net Effective at Fighting Poverty, But Has Weakened for the Very Poorest," Center on Budget and Policy Priorities, July 6, 2009. For 2010, Sherman calculated that the poverty rate would be 28.6 percent and that 38.4 million more people would be poor in the absence of public benefits, including benefits added temporarily by the Recovery Act. Arloc Sherman, "Without the Safety Net, More Than a Quarter of Americans Would Have Been Poor Last Year," *Off the Charts* blog, Center on Budget and Policy Priorities, November 9, 2011, www.offthechartsblog.org/without-the-safety-net-more-than-a -quarter-of-americans-would-have-been-poor-last-year/.

3. Paul N. Van de Water and Arloc Sherman, "Social Security Keeps 20 million Americans Out of Poverty: A State-By-State Analysis," Center on Budget and Policy Priorities, August 11, 2010.

4. George H.W. Bush, commencement address at the University of Michigan Graduation Ceremonies, May 4, 1991, Weekly Compilation of Presidential Documents, vol. 27, p. 563.

5. Lyndon Johnson, "Remarks at the University of Michigan Graduation Ceremonies," May 22, 1964, 1963–64 Public Papers, part 1, p. 704.

3. Why Are We Stuck?

1. Carmen DeNavas-Walt et al., *Income, Poverty, and Health Insurance Coverage in the United States: 2009*, Current Population Reports (Washington, DC: U.S. Government Printing Office, 2010), 14, fig. 4.

2. Ibid.

3. U.S. Department of Housing and Urban Development, *The 2010 Annual Homeless Assessment Report to Congress* (Washington, DC: U.S. Department of Housing and Urban Development, 2010), www.hudhre.info/documents/2010Ho melessAssessmentReport.pdf.

4. Paul Taylor, Rakesh Kochhar, and Richard Fry, *Wealth Gaps Rise to Record Highs Between Whites, Blacks and Hispanics* (Washington, DC: Pew Research Center, June 26, 2011), pewsocialtrends.org/files/2011/07/SDT-Wealth-Report _7-26-11_FINAL.pdf.

5. Children's Defense Fund, *The State of America's Children 2011* (Washington, DC: Children's Defense Fund, July 18, 2011), B-2, www.childrensdefense.org/ child-research-data-publications/data/state-of-americas-2011.pdf. Other facts cited in the report include: "The number of children in poverty increased 28 percent between 2000 and 2009 after dropping 27 percent between 1992 and 2000. Child poverty increased by almost 10 percent between 2008 and 2009, the largest single-year increase since 1960. Children of color continue to suffer disproportionately from poverty. Black and Hispanic children are about three times as likely to be poor as White non-Hispanic children."

6. DeNavas-Walt et al., *Income, Poverty, and Health Insurance Coverage*, 55.

7. Rebecca M. Blank and Mark H. Greenberg, *Improving the Measurement of Poverty* (Washington, DC: Brookings Institution, December 2008), 6, www.brook ings.edu/~/media/Files/rc/papers/2008/12_poverty_measurement_blank/12_pov erty_measurement_blank.pdf.

8. U.S. Census Bureau, "Tables of NAS-Based Poverty Estimates: 2009," February 16, 2011, www.census.gov/hhes/povmeas/data/nas/tables/2009/index.html.

9. Kathleen Short, "The Research Supplemental Poverty Measure: 2010," U.S. Census Bureau, November 2011; Sabrina Tavernese and Robert Gebeloff, "New Way to Tally Poor Recasts View of Poverty," *New York Times*, November 1, 2011. The poverty line for a family of four under the SPM was $24,343 in 2010 (with adjustments for regional variations in income), as opposed to $22,113 under the official measure. The SPM adds SNAP, the school lunch program; WIC (the Supplementary Nutrition Program for Women, Infants, and Children); housing subsidies; and LIHEAP (Low-Income Home Energy Assistance) to income and subtracts taxes (but adds the EITC and other credits), work-related expenses, child care expenses, medical out-of-pocket expenses, and child support paid.

10. Heather Boushey et al., *Hardships in America: The Real Story of Working Families* (Washington, DC: Economic Policy Institute, 2001).

11. Wider Opportunities for Women, *The Basic Economic Security Tables for the United States* (Washington, DC: Wider Opportunities for Women, 2010), www.wowonline.org/documents/BESTIndexforTheUnitedStates2010.pdf.

12. Sabrina Tavernese, "Outside Cleveland, Snapshots of Poverty's Surge in the Suburbs," *New York Times*, October 25, 2011.

13. U.S. Census Bureau, *Annual Social and Economic Supplement*, Current Population Survey, 2010, table POV27-001.

14. Half in Ten, *Top 10 Findings from Half in Ten's Inaugural Report Tracking Our Progress Reducing Poverty* (Washington, DC: Center for American Progress, October 26, 2011).

15. Julia B. Isaacs, Isabel V. Sawhill, and Ron Haskins, *Getting Ahead or Losing Ground: Economic Mobility in America* (Washington, DC: Brookings Institution Press, 2008), 76.

16. Lawrence Mishel, Jared Bernstein, and Heidi Shierholz, *The State of Working America 2008/2009* (Ithaca, NY: ILA Press/Economic Policy Institute, 2009).

17. Isaacs, Sawhill, and Haskins, *Getting Ahead or Losing Ground*, 52, 75.

18. Robert Pear, "It's Official: The Rich Get Richer," *New York Times*, October 26, 2011.

19. Isabel V. Sawhill and John E. Morton, *Economic Mobility: Is the American Dream Alive and Well?* (Washington, DC: Economic Mobility Project, 2007), 3.

20. Heather Boushey and Christian E. Weller, "What the Numbers Tell Us," in *Inequality Matters: The Growing Economic Divide in America and Its Poisonous Consequences*, ed. James Lardner and David Smith (New York: The New Press, 2005).

21. Avi Feller and Chad Stone, *Top 1 percent of Americans Reaped Two-Thirds of Income Gains in Last Expansion* (Washington, DC: Center on Budget and Policy Priorities, September 9, 2009).

22. U.S. Census Bureau, *Annual Social and Economic Supplement*.

23. Ibid.

24. Arloc Sherman, "Safety Net Effective at Fighting Poverty but Has Weakened for the Very Poorest," Center for Budget and Policy Priorities, July 6, 2009.

25. Stockholm International Peace Research Institute, "SIPRI Military Expenditure Database," 2010, www.sipri.org/databases/milex.

26. U.S. Census Bureau, *Annual Social and Economic Supplement*.

27. Joyce A. Martin et al., *Births: Final Data for 2008*, National Vital Statistics Reports (Hyattsville, MD: National Center for Health Statistics, December 8, 2010), 21, table 1.

28. David T. Ellwood and Christopher Jencks, "The Uneven Spread of Single-Parent Families: What Do We Know? Where Do We Look for Answers?" in *Social Inequality*, ed. Kathryn M. Neckerman (New York: Russell Sage Foundation, 2004), 17, fig. 1.9.

29. Stephanie J. Ventura, *Changing Patterns of Nonmarital Childbearing in the United States*, NCHS data brief (Hyattsville, MD: National Center for Health Statistics, May 2009), 5, fig. 6.

30. Martin et al., *Births: Final Data for 2008*, 21, table 1.

31. Stephanie J. Ventura et al., "The Demography of Out-of-Wedlock Child-bearing," in *Report to Congress on Out-of-Wedlock Childbearing* (Hyattsville, MD: National Center for Health Statistics, 1995), 10, fig. II-1; Martin et al., *Births: Final Data for 2008*, 47, table 16.

32. Ventura, *Changing Patterns of Nonmarital Childbearing in the United States*, 2.

33. Sara McLanahan, "Fragile Families and the Reproduction of Poverty," *Annals of the American Academy of Political and Social Science* 621, no. 1 (January 2009): 112.

34. Ellwood and Jencks, "Uneven Spread of Single-Parent Families," 47–48.

35. William Julius Wilson, *The Truly Disadvantaged: The Inner City, the Under-class, and Public Policy* (Chicago: University of Chicago Press, 1987).

36. See McLanahan, "Fragile Families and the Reproduction of Poverty," 116.

37. Kathryn L.S. Pettit and G. Thomas Kingsley, *Concentrated Poverty: A Change in Course* (Washington, DC: Urban Institute, 2003), www.urban.org/Up loadedPDF/310790_NCUA2.pdf.

38. U.S. Census Bureau, *Annual Social and Economic Supplement*.

4. Jobs: The Economy and Public Policy Go South (for Most of Us)

1. See James Tobin, "It Can Be Done! Conquering Poverty in the US by 1976," *New Republic*, June 3, 1967, 14–18.

2. Ibid., 16.

3. Ibid., 18.

4. Claudia Goldin and Lawrence F. Katz, "Long-Run Changes in the Wage Structure: Narrowing, Widening, Polarizing," *Brookings Papers on Economic Activity* 2 (Washington, DC: Brookings Institution, 2007), 135.

5. Lawrence Mishel, Jared Bernstein, and Heidi Shierholz, *The State of Working America 2008/2009* (Ithaca, NY: ILR Press/Economic Policy Institute, 2009).

6. Frank Levy and Peter Temin, "Inequality and Institutions in 20th Century America," working paper, MIT, Cambridge, MA, June 27, 2007, 31–32.

7. Economic Policy Institute, "The Real Value of the Minimum Wage, 1960–2010," www.stateofworkingamerica.org/files/images/orig/Wages_minwage.png.

8. Lane Kenworthy, "Low Wage Jobs and No Wage Growth: Is There a Way Out?" New America Foundation, June 2011, growth.newamerica.net/sites/newamerica.net/files/policydocs/Kenworthy.pdf.

9. See Jacob Hacker and Paul Pierson, *Winner-Take-All Politics* (New York: Simon & Schuster, 2011), 129–31.

10. Ibid., 99.

11. See Barry Hirsch, "Sluggish Institutions in a Dynamic World: Can Unions and Industrial Competition Coexist?" *Journal of Economic Perspectives* 22, no. 1 (2008): 153–76.

12. Ibid., 161.

13. Jefferson Cowie, *Stayin' Alive: The 1970s and the Last Days of the Working Class* (New York: The New Press, 2010), 2.

14. Leo Troy and Neil Sheflin, *U.S. Union Sourcebook* (IRDIS, 1985).

15. Bureau of Labor Statistics, "Union Members—2010," January 21, 2011, www.bls.gov/news.release/pdf/union2.pdf.

16. Hirsch, "Sluggish Institutions in a Dynamic World," 156; Bureau of Labor Statistics, "Union Members—2010."

17. See Francine Blau and Lawrence Kahn, "International Differences in Male Wage Inequality: Institutional versus Market Forces," *Journal of Political Economy* 104, no. 4 (1996): 791–837.

18. David Card and Alan B. Krueger, *Myth and Measurement: The New Economics of the Minimum Wage* (Princeton: Princeton University Press: 1995), 277–79.

19. David Card and Alan B. Krueger, "Minimum Wages and Employment: A Case Study of the Fast Food Industry in New Jersey and Pennsylvania," *American Economic Review*, September 1994, 772.

20. See David Neumark and William Wascher, "Minimum Wages and Low-Wage Workers: How Well Does Reality Match the Rhetoric?" *Minnesota Law Review* 92 (2008): 1296–316.

21. House Committee on Financial Services Committee, *Conduct of Monetary Policy: Hearing Before the Committee on Financial Services*, 107th Cong., 1st sess., July 18, 2001, 14.

22. Heather Boushey, "The New Breadwinners," in *The Shriver Report: A Woman's Nation Changes Everything*, ed. Heather Boushey and Ann O'Leary (Washington, DC: Center For American Progress, 2009), 33.

23. Ibid., 35.

24. Ibid., 32.

25. Timothy Grall, *Custodial Mothers and Fathers and Their Child Support: 2007* (Washington, DC: U.S. Department of Congress, 2007), 9.

26. See George J. Borjas, Richard B. Freeman, Lawrence F. Katz, John DiNardo, and John M. Abowd, "How Much Do Immigration and Trade Affect Labor Market Outcomes?" *Brookings Papers on Economic Activity* 1997, no. 1 (1997): 5–9.

27. Ibid., 65.

28. George Borjas, "The Labor Demand Curve Is Downward Sloping: Reexamining the Impact of Immigration on the Labor Market," *Quarterly Journal of Economics* 118, no. 4 (2003): 1335–74.

29. David Card, "Is the New Immigration Really So Bad?" *Economic Journal* 115, no. 4 (2005): F300–F323.

30. David Autor, David Dorn, and Gordon Hanson, "The China Syndrome: Local Labor Market Effects of Import Competition in the United States," working paper, MIT, Cambridge, MA, June 2011, 18.

31. Claudia Goldin and Lawrence Katz, *The Race Between Education and Technology* (Cambridge, MA: Belknap Press of Harvard University Press, 2008), 4.

32. Remarks Prepared for Delivery by Treasury Secretary Henry H. Paulson at Columbia University, August 1, 2006.

33. Ibid.

34. Nick Taylor, *American-Made: When FDR Put the Nation to Work* (New York: Bantam Dell, 2009), 541–49.

35. Charles B. Blow, "They, Too, Sing America," *New York Times*, July 16, 2011.

36. Harry J. Holzer and Robert I. Lerman, "The Future of Middle-Skill Jobs," brief 41, Center on Children and Families, 2009, 3–7; see also Harry J. Holzer and Robert I. Lerman, "America's Forgotten Middle-Skill Jobs: Education and Training Requirements in the Next Decade and Beyond," working paper, Workforce Alliance, Washington, DC, 2007.

37. Karen Martinson, Alexandra Stanczyk, and Lauren Eyster, "Low-Skill Workers Access to Quality Green Jobs," brief 13, Urban Institute, Washington, DC, 2010.

38. Ibid., 1.

39. Kyle Boyd, "The Color of Help: Workers of Color Dominate Domestic Services but Lack Union Rights," Center for American Progress, June 17, 2011, www.americanprogress.org/issues/2011/06/color_of_help.html.

40. Annette Bernhardt et al., *Broken Laws, Unprotected Workers: Violations of Employment and Labor Laws in America's Cities* (New York: Center for Urban Economic Development at UIC, 2008), www.nelp.org/page/-/brokenlaws/Broken LawsReport2009.pdf.

41. Scott Martelle, *Confronting the Gloves-Off Economy* (Chicago: Labor and Employment Relations Association, 2009), 3.

42. Bernhardt et al., *Broken Laws, Unprotected Workers*.

43. U.S. Government Accountability Office, *Fair Labor Standards Act: Better Use of Available Resources and Consistent Reporting Could Improve Compliance*, GAO-08-962T, July 15, 2008, 1.

44. National Employment Law Project, *Winning Wage Justice: An Advocate's Guide to State and City Policies to Fight Wage Theft* (New York: National Employment Law Project, 2011), 41.

45. See Just Pay Working Group, *Just Pay: Improving Wage and Hour Enforcement at the United States Department of Labor* (New York: National Employment Law Project, 2011).

46. See Hacker and Pierson, *Winner-Take-All Politics*, 60, 270, 278–79.

47. Until the end of 2012, the EITC adds $5,751 to the income of a minimum-wage worker with three children. This provision was added temporarily as part of the Recovery Act in 2009.

48. "Preview of 2011 EITC Income Limits, Maximum Credit Amounts and Tax Law Updates," Internal Revenue Service, www.irs.gov/individuals/article/ 0,,id=233839,00.html.

49. See Center for American Progress Task Force on Poverty, *From Poverty to Prosperity: A National Strategy to Cut Poverty in Half* (Washington, DC: Center for American Progress, 2007) 27–29.

50. See Peter Edelman, Harry Holzer, and Paul Offner, *Reconnecting Disadvantaged Young Men* (Washington, DC: Urban Institute Press, 2006).

51. See "Child Tax Credit: Publication 972," Internal Revenue Service, www .irs.gov/pub/irs-pdf/p972.pdf.

52. See Her Majesty's Treasury, *The Child and Working Tax Credits: The Modernisation of Britain's Tax and Benefit System* (London: HM Treasury, 2002).

53. See Congressional Budget Office, "Letter to the Honorable Nancy Pelosi Providing an Analysis of the Reconciliation Proposal," March 20, 2010.

54. Text of President Nixon's veto message of the Child Development Act of 1971, *Congressional Record*, December 10, 1971, 46057–59.

55. See Center for American Progress Task Force on Poverty, *From Poverty to Prosperity: A National Strategy to Cut Poverty in Half* (Washington, DC: Center for American Progress, 2007) 31–33.

56. National Low Income Housing Coalition, *Out of Reach 2011* (Washington, DC: National Low Income Housing Coalition, 2011), 1.

57. Ibid., 6.

5. Deep Poverty: A Gigantic Hole in the Safety Net

1. Arloc Sherman, "Safety Net Effective at Fighting Poverty but Has Weakened for the Very Poorest," Center on Budget and Policy Priorities, July 6, 2009, www.cbpp.org/files/7-6-09pov.pdf; Jason DeParle, Robert Gebeloff, and Sabrina Tavernise, "Experts Say Bleak Portrait of Poverty Missed the Mark," *New York Times*, November 4, 2011.

2. Note, by the way, that the Census poverty figures do not include homeless people at all. Nor do they include low-income seniors in nursing homes, whose basic needs are frequently paid for by Medicaid. (Most poverty measures, including Sherman's, don't count Medicaid benefits as income, because experts feel they can't be used in any predictable way to pay everyday bills.)

3. Southern Education Foundation, *Update: Worst of Times: Extreme Poverty in the United States, 2009* (Atlanta: Southern Education Foundation, December 22, 2010), www.sefatl.org/pdf/Extreme%20Poverty-%20Update-12-21-10.pdf.

4. U.S. Department of Health and Human Services, "TANF—Caseload Data."

5. U.S. Department of Health and Human Services, *Indicators of Welfare Dependence, Annual Report to Congress, 2008*, table IND 4a, aspe.hhs.gov/hsp/indicators08/index.shtml.

6. Jim Kaminski, *Trends in Welfare Caseloads* (Washington, DC: Urban Institute, n.d.), www.urban.org/uploadedpdf/TANF_caseload.pdf.

7. Kristin Seefeldt, "When Ends Don't Meet: Debt and Its Role in Low-Income Women's Economic Coping Strategies," forthcoming in 2011.

8. Sheila R. Zedlewski et al., *Families Coping Without Earnings or Government Cash Assistance*, Assessing the New Federalism (Washington, DC: Urban Institute, February 2003), www.urban.org/UploadedPDF/410634_OP64.pdf.

9. Heather Hill and Jacqueline Kauff, *Living on Little: Case Studies of Iowa Families with Very Low Incomes* (Princeton, NJ: Mathematica Policy Research, August 2001), www.mathematica-mpr.com/PDFs/liveonlittle.pdf.

10. LaDonna Pavetti, "Welfare Reform Not the 'Success' Ryan Claims," *Off the Charts* blog, Center on Budget and Policy Priorities, May 25, 2011, www.offthechartsblog.org/welfare-reform-not-the-%E2%80%9Csuccess%E2%80%9D-ryan-claims/.

11. Gregory Acs, Pamela Loprest, and Tracy Roberts, *Final Synthesis Report of Findings from ASPE'S "Leavers" Grants* (Washington, DC: Urban Institute, November 27, 2001), 24, www.urban.org/UploadedPDF/410809_welfare_leavers_synthesis.pdf.

12. Gretchen Rowe, Mary Murphy, and Ei Yin Mon, *Welfare Rules Databook: State TANF Policies as of July 2009* (Washington, DC: Urban Institute, August 2010), 114, table III.B.3, anfdata.urban.org/databooks/Databook%202009%20FINAL.pdf.

13. Pamela Loprest and Sheila Zedlewski, *The Changing Role of Welfare in the Lives of Low-Income Families with Children* (Washington, DC: Urban Institute, August 2006), www.urban.org/publications/311357.html.

14. Greg J. Duncan and Katherine Magnuson, "The Long Reach of Early Childhood Poverty," *Pathways*, Winter 2011, www.stanford.edu/group/scspi/_media/pdf/pathways/winter_2011/PathwaysWinter11_Duncan.pdf.

6. Concentrated Poverty: "The Abandoned"

1. Eugene Robinson, *Disintegration: The Splintering of Black America* (New York: Doubleday, 2010).

2. Kathryn L.S. Pettit and G. Thomas Kingsley, *Concentrated Poverty: A Change in Course* (Washington, DC: Urban Institute, May 2003), www.urban.org/UploadedPDF/310790_NCUA2.pdf.

3. Elizabeth Kneebone, Carey Nadeau, and Alan Berube, *The Re-Emergence of Concentrated Poverty: Metropolitan Trends in the 2000s* (Washington, DC: Brookings Institution, November 2011).

4. Ibid.

5. Alemayehu Bishaw, *Areas with Concentrated Poverty: 1999*, Census 2000 Special Reports (Washington, DC: U.S. Census Bureau, July 2005), www.census.gov/prod/2005pubs/censr-16.pdf.

6. SANDAG, "Population and Housing Estimates, City Heights Community Planning Area," August 2010, profilewarehouse.sandag.org/profiles/est/sdcpa1456est.pdf.

7. Robert F. Kennedy, *RFK: Collected Speeches* (New York: Viking, 1993), 167.

8. *Philadelphia Empowerment Zone 1995–2005* (Philadelphia: Philadelphia Empowerment Zone, May 2006).

9. Alexander Polikoff, "HOPE VI and the Deconcentration of Poverty," in *From Despair to Hope: HOPE VI and the New Promise of Public Housing in America's Cities*, ed. Henry G. Cisneros and Lora Engdahl (Washington, DC: Brookings Institution Press, 2009), 72, fig. 5-5.

10. Ibid., 70.

11. Bruce Katz, "The Origins of HOPE VI," in Cisneros and Engdahl, *From Despair to Hope*, 15.

12. Sheila Crowley, "HOPE VI: What Went Wrong," in Cisneros and Engdahl, *From Despair to Hope*, 229.

13. Kennedy, *RFK*, 176.

7. Young People: Improving the Odds

1. David T. Burkam and Valerie E. Lee, *Inequality at the Starting Gate: Social Background Differences in Achievement as Children Begin School* (Washington DC: Economic Policy Institute, 2002).

2. Donald J. Hernandez, "Double Jeopardy: How Third-Grade Reading Skills and Poverty Influence High School Graduation," Annie E. Casey Foundation, April 2011.

3. Christopher Hartney and Fabiana Silva, "And Justice for Some: Differential Treatment of Youth of Color in the Justice System," National Council on Crime and Delinquency, January 2007, 1.

4. Michelle Alexander, *The New Jim Crow: Mass Incarceration in the Age of Colorblindness* (New York: The New Press, 2010).

5. Heather C. West, "Prison and Jail Inmates at Midyear 2009" (No. NCJ 230113), Bureau of Justice Statistics, Washington, DC, 2009.

6. Todd D. Minton, "Jail Inmates at Midyear 2010—Statistical Tables," Bureau of Justice Statistics, Washington, DC, 2010.

7. U.S. Government Accounting Office, "Report to the Chairman, Committee on Education and Labor, House of Representatives: Disconnected Youth: Federal Action Could Address Some of the Challenges Faced by Local Programs That Reconnect Youth to Education and Employment," February 2008, 5–6.

8. Andrew Sum et al., *Left Behind in the Labor Market: Labor Market Problems of the Nation's Out-of-School, Young Adult Populations* (Boston: Northeastern University, Center for Labor Market Studies, 2003), 9.

9. U.S. Government Accounting Office, "Report to the Chairman, Committee on Education and Labor, House of Representatives: Disconnected Youth," 6.

10. YTFG, "Understanding Transition Points," www.ytfg.org/knowledge.

11. Gary Orfield, ed., *Dropouts in America: Confronting the Graduation Rate Crisis* (Cambridge, MA: Harvard Education Press, 2004), 1.

12. Michael Wald and Tia Martinez, "Connected by 25: Improving the Life Chances of the Country's Most Vulnerable 14–24 Year Olds," William and Flora Hewlett Foundation Working Paper, November, 2003, 7.

13. Tony Fabelo, Michael D. Thompson, and Martha Plotkin, "Breaking Schools' Rules: A Statewide Study of How School Discipline Relates to Students' Success and Juvenile Justice Involvement," Council of State Governments Justice Center in partnership with the Public Policy Research Institute at Texas A&M University, July 2011, 45.

14. Anthony P. Carnevale, Nicole Smith, and Jeff Strohl, "Help Wanted: Projections of Jobs and Education Requirements Through 2018," Georgetown Center on Education and the Workforce, June 2010, 13.

15. Ibid., 26.

16. Ibid., 106.

17. NAF, "About NAF," naf.org/about-naf.

18. James J. Kemple, "Career Academies: Impacts on Labor Market Outcomes an Educational Attainment," Manpower Demonstration Research Corporation, New York, March 2004, ES-9.

19. James J. Kemple and Jason C. Snipes, "Career Academies Impacts on Students' Engagement and Performance in High School," Manpower Demonstration Research Corporation, New York, February 2000, 47.

20. Kemple, "Career Academies: Impacts on Labor Market Outcomes and Educational Attainment," 16.

21. James J. Kemple and Cynthia J. Willner, "Career Academies: Long-Term Impacts on Labor Market Outcomes, Educational Attainment, and Transitions to Adulthood," Manpower Demonstration Research Corporation, New York, 2008, 17.

22. Alison L. Fraser, "Vocational-Technical Education in Massachusetts," Pioneer Institute White Paper, No. 42, October 2008, 6.

23. Ibid., 8.

24. Gateway to College, 2010 Annual Report, 2011, www.gatewaytocollege.org/pdf/2010%20Annual%20Report.pdf.

25. Lili Allen and Rebecca E. Wolfe, "Back on Track to College: A Texas School District Leverages State Policy to Put Dropouts on the Path to Success," Jobs for the Future, September 2010, 5, www.jff.org/sites/default/files/BackOnTrackCCTA-091510.pdf.

26. Cheryl Almeida, Cassius Johnson, and Adria Steinberg, "Making Good on a Promise: What Policymakers Can Do to Support the Educational Persistence of Dropouts," Jobs for the Future, April 2006, 3.

27. YouthBuild USA, "About YouthBuild," www.youthbuild.org/site/c.htIRI3PIKoG/b.1223921/k.BD3C/Home.htm.

28. YouthBuild USA, "10,000 Students and Workers Lose Educational Opportunities and Jobs," press release, May 18, 2011, www.youthbuild.org/site/apps/nl/newsletter2.asp?b=1286765&c=htIRI3PIKoG.

29. YouthBuild USA, "About Us," www.youthbuild.org/site/c.htIRI3PIKoG/b.1223923/k.C7D6/About_Us.htm.

30. YouthBuild, "Effective Local Youth Programs Lose Federal Funding—More Than 120 YouthBuild Programs Face Funding Loss, Possible Closure," press release, May 18, 2011, www.youthbuild.org/site/apps/nlnet/content2.aspx?c=htIRI3PIKoG&b=1321681&ct=10884369&notoc=1.

31. YouthBuild USA, "YouthBuild Demographics and Outcomes," www.youthbuild.org/site/c.htIRI3PIKoG/b.1418407/k.6738/YouthBuild_Demographics_and_Outcomes.htm.

32. The Corps Network, "Service and Conservation Corps," www.corpsnetwork.org/index.php?option=com_content&view=article&id=84&Itemid=64.

33. David Bornstein, "Training Youths in the Ways of the Workplace," New York Times, January 4, 2011, opinionator.blogs.nytimes.com/2011/01/24/an-education-in-the-ways-of-the-workplace/.

34. "Mayor Bloomberg Launches Nation's Most Comprehensive Effort to Tackle Disparities Between Young Black and Latino Males and Their Peers," press release, August 4, 2011, www.nyc.gov/html/om/html/2011b/pr282-11.html.

35. Anne Roder and Mark Elliott, "A Promising Start: Year Up's Initial Impacts on Low-Income Young Adults' Careers," Economic Mobility Corporation, New York, April 2011, 1.

INDEX

public housing, 75, 108, 121–23.
    See also housing vouchers
public policy
    current state of, xiii
    importance of, xviii
    need for change in, 81
    skepticism about, xv
    support for, 99
    See also specific headings
public service jobs, 61

race, xvii, 30–31, 41–45
racism, 45, 101
Rangel, Charles, 115, 116
Reagan, Ronald
    anecdote about "welfare queens,"
        41, 43
    anti-welfare campaign under, 44,
        86
    appointments to National Labor
        Relations Board by, 51
    child care legislation under, 74
    on poverty, 14
    proposal of food stamps cuts, 12
    tax reform bill signed by, 21
recession, xiii, xix
    effects of, 25
    role of welfare in, 93
Recovery Act. *See* American
    Recovery and Reinvestment Act
Rector, Robert, 4, 5
refundable tax credits, 71
Rendell, Ed, 117–18
Republican Party, 43, 77
residential patterns, 120, 131–32
responsibility, personal, 102–3
restaurant jobs, 61
Robinson, Eugene, 101
Roe v. Wade, 51, 77
role models, 104
Roosevelt, Franklin D., 59, 60, 76,
    84
Rouse, James, 111, 114
rural poverty, 29

"safety net," 80, 84, 92, 161
San Diego, California, 128–29
Sandtown-Winchester neighborhood
    (Baltimore), 111, 125–27
SBTC (skill-biased technological
    change theory), 57–58
Schakowsky, Jan, 60
school systems. *See* education
Schorr, Daniel, 8–9
Seefeldt, Kristin, 90, 91
segregation, 108, 109, 131
Service Employees International
    Union (SEIU), 66, 68, 69
service jobs, 49
Shalala, Donna, xii, 116
Sherman, Arloc, 81–83, 97
Sherman Antitrust Act, 76
Shriver, R. Sargent, 15
single-parent families
    deep poverty of, 83
    and Earned Income Tax Credit,
        71–72
    increase in, xvii
    See also female-headed families
60 Minutes (TV show), 99
skill-biased technological change
    theory (SBTC), 57–58
skilled crafts, 61
SNAP. *See* Supplemental Nutrition
    Assistance Program
social mobility, 160
Social Security Act, xv, 116
Social Security payments, 29, 82
Soros, George, 156
Southern United States, 83
Southwestern United States, 106
SPM (Supplemental Poverty
    Measure)
    development of, 28
    middle class in, 29
SSI (Supplementary Security
    Income)
    creation of, 43
    effects of, xvi